What People Are Saying...

"...It answers so many questions – Lisa's understanding of the disease, her understanding of codependency and the way she presents it – it's just really a fine piece of work!"

Caroll Fowler, M.A., MFT,
*Retired Director of the Family
Program at The Sequoia Center*

"WOW...it took me years to know and countless books to read what you have put into one compact and fact-filled book. It's a sincere, down-to-earth account of what you and many others have experienced and for those still suffering, a 'bible' to live their life by."

Joan Ryan

"Wow, even after 14 years in recovery, I was stunned by how much I learned from Lisa's book. She provides straight-talking explanations of alcoholism, alcohol abuse, alcohol use, underage drinking and more. I've never found a book like this one. Short and to the point, reads like a novel, packed with information and hope. It's sure to help anyone who has a loved one who drinks too much."

Joan A.

"If You Loved Me, You'd Stop!" does not pretend to have all the answers. Rather, its focus is to help you think about the issues involved when someone you love has a problem with alcohol. . ."*

Cathy Fleischman, RN, MSN

"If You Loved Me, You'd Stop! is about g) of
an alcoholic survive and move forwa their
dignity intact." hnston

IF YOU LOVED ME, YOU'D STOP! YOU'D STOP!

WHAT YOU *REALLY* NEED TO KNOW WHEN YOUR LOVED ONE DRINKS TOO MUCH

BY
LISA FREDERIKSEN

 **PUBLISHING**

MENLO PARK, CA
www.kljpublishing.com

KLJ Publishing
Menlo Park, CA
www.kljpublishing.com

Printed in the United States of America

ISBN: 978-0-9816844-0-6

Library of Congress Control Number: 2008906340

WARNING AND DISCLAIMER
The purpose of this book is to provide information. Every effort has been made to make this book as accurate as possible, but no warrant of fitness is implied. The information provided is on an "as is" basis. The author and the publisher shall have neither liability nor responsibility to any person or entity with respect to any injury, loss or damage caused or alleged to have been caused, directly or indirectly, by the information contained in this book. Additionally, the memoir-type pieces interspersed throughout are the author's perspective and remembrance, and she fully appreciates and accepts others may have different perspectives and remembrances of the same events. These memoir-type pieces are shared solely to help frame the larger issues – namely, the dynamics and coping behaviors that are adopted by individuals in families where alcoholism and/or alcohol abuse are present but not understood nor effectively discussed.

Dedicated To

the tens of millions of people whose lives are
or have been affected by a loved one's drinking,

and

my daughters, Jessica Erin and Kathryn Marie,
for their courage, strength, love and support.

Table of Contents

Bibliography ....

Endnotes ....

IF YOU
LOVED ME,
YOU'D STOP!

WHAT YOU *REALLY* NEED TO KNOW WHEN
YOUR LOVED ONE DRINKS TOO MUCH

CHAPTER 1

"If You Loved Me, You'd STOP!"

"If you loved me, you'd stop!" How many times have you said, pleaded or screamed these words at your husband, brother or daughter after a particularly nasty bout of drinking? How many times has your wife, sister or son promised to stop or cut down…drink no more than two a day…drink only on the week-ends? How many times has your heart been broken when *this* time turned out to be just like all of the times before?

Those of us who love someone – a spouse, child, parent or friend – whose drinking has become an all-consuming problem in our own lives – will likely have spent years trying to fix things. That's why we'd pick up a book with a title like this one. We are desperate.

I understand. I was desperate, too, because I've had (and have) loved ones who drink too much. I was desperate for an answer to the question I'd churned over and over in my mind for years: "Why? – Why, if they love me – why won't they stop the drinking that is ruining our lives?"

I was sure that if I could just find the answer, if I could just leverage their love for me, I could make them stop – or at least limit their drinking to a level *I* considered acceptable. I believed, like tens of millions (yes, tens of millions!) of other wives, husbands, parents, children and siblings who love someone who drinks too much, that I had the power to help my loved ones get a grip on their drinking and in so doing, return our lives to normal. And so I spent years trying to roll back the present to a time past – a time that had started out so happily – until I was consumed with anger and frustration, as each "last time" became the new next.

In the end, I learned alcoholics can't stop their problem drinking as long as they consume <u>any</u> amount of alcohol. I learned that as long as they even think they can drink successfully at some time in the future, there is no amount of willpower nor good intentions in the world that can help them avoid a "next time." I learned about a whole other "stage" of drinking called alcohol abuse. Alcohol abuse is the term used to describe the various forms of excessive drinking that cause significant risk, harm and distress to the excessive drinker and to his or her family and friends[1] – risk, harm and distress equal to that which is associated with the disease of alcoholism (DUIs, arrests, school, family and work relationship problems).

It took me a while and a lot of research, therapy and recovery work to finally understand the simple fact that when excessive drinking crosses the line from alcohol abuse to alcohol addiction – it's then a full-blown disease, the disease of alcoholism (a subject covered in Chapters 2 and 3). In the process, I learned so much more about so many other issues related to my loved ones' drinking and my reactions to it. Which brings me to my loved ones.

In order to protect their privacy, I will not be speaking about any loved one in particular, as there have been several – both friends and family – male and female – whose collective drinking behaviors have included countless broken promises to stop or cut down, DUIs (driving while under the influence), arrests, health issues, financial problems, lost friendships, bankruptcy, "disappearing acts," insane circular arguments about what constituted "excessive drinking," verbal abuse and even physical intimidation and violence. Rather, I will use a composite. My composite's name will be Alex (or loved one), and I will use the pronoun "he" for simplicity's sake. At times, I will refer to them all collectively as "loved ones." But Alex is a composite, and the scenarios I attribute to Alex are drawn from assorted experiences I've had with one or more of them at various times over the years.

With this understanding, I invite you to read what I've learned – information that had I known years ago would have completely changed the way I've lived my life and related to my loved ones and their drinking. This book provides you with the most current brain research on alcoholism, excessive drinking and addiction, as well as the latest research on the issues surrounding the disease of alcoholism and the condition of alcohol abuse. I've done my best to present this information in easy-to-understand terms, and I've included footnotes and appendices of resources to help clarify some of the more complex issues.

This book also gives you suggestions for changing your own behavior – something you can't imagine needing to do right now – after all, he (or she) has the problem! Yet, it will likely be these suggestions that will make your life more tolerable, whether your loved one stops drinking or not, whether you continue the relationship or end it. I can make this claim because not only did I survive the decades of devastation my various loved ones' alcoholism and alcohol abuse has caused in my life, ultimately I've thrived!

If You Loved Me, You'd Stop!

And you can too. For by the time I finally began my own road to understanding, I was one angry, frustrated, resentful person. The more Alex drank or broke his promises not to drink or to cut back on his drinking, the more vigilant I'd become. I knew the next "fix" would be the one that would finally work. When that didn't happen, I would step up my efforts – admonishing, nagging, pleading, arguing, crying, pouting, ignoring, and so on. My common theme was, "If you loved me, you'd stop!"

I honestly believed and figured that if I just managed our household more efficiently or did a better job of scheduling activities or _____ (fill in the blank, I'm sure I tried it), then he'd quit drinking so much and our lives would finally be happy. And, when I couldn't control his drinking, I'd step up my vigilance to manage the next inevitable crisis as a way of wresting control of the situation – and in a complex life of marriage, jobs, children, ex-spouses, friends and family, there was an endless source and variety. Little did I understand that focusing on the next crisis was a way of trying to control some aspect of my life, but in fact, it often created problems of a different nature (like my daughter setting aside her own needs in order to make me happy when she sensed I was upset with Alex, for example). But, as long as I focused "over there," I didn't have to face the underlying problem right in front of me – alcohol – Alex's use of it and my reactions to his use.

For you see, unknowingly at the time, I was living in the dangerous world of "enmeshment" – the place where I had absolutely no concept of boundaries. I didn't know where "I" ended and "someone else" (Alex, for example) began. In my world, the "I" and the "someone else" were one and the same. My identity was thoroughly entangled in the notion that it was my job to make sure others were happy, toed the line and succeeded at work, in school and life in general. It was my job to see the world as others saw it or to make sure they saw it the way I did. I'd reduced my world to rigid absolutes – good or bad, right or wrong, the truth or a lie – because with absolutes, there was a target, an objective, something that could be argued and fought for until a "winner" and a "loser" could be declared. And, by gosh, I was going to "win" this battle over my loved one's drinking or the next crisis because my whole being was caught up in what others thought of me. If "they" (whomever "they" were) thought I was good or right, then I was good or right.

Luckily for me, Alex entered a treatment program, which plunged me into a whole other world – a world that included terms and concepts like codependency, adult children of alcoholics, 12-step programs, co-addictions, dual diagnosis and the role a family member has in the denial that protects a loved one's drinking. It was a world I found confusing and overwhelming.

True to my nature, I began my quest for deeper understanding in the same way I'd approached my other published books and articles. I immersed myself in research, intent on learning as much as I could about the subject – in this case alcoholism and treatment programs – and then all of the other issues which emerged as I tried to understand why a loved one drinks too much and why someone like myself puts up with it for so long. I started attending Al-Anon[1] meetings and doubled my individual therapy sessions. Additionally, I was extremely fortunate Alex had chosen a treatment program that had a family-help component as part of its effort to help the alcoholic. I took part in their weekly family group sessions and added additional weekly sessions, as well.

Keeping the focus on myself in this manner keeps me from unraveling as my life continues to take new twists and turns. Now, it's different. I still experience anger, shock, fear and disbelief and can go down paths that aren't very productive, but now, in these times, I am also armed with knowledge and a sense of self I'd previously not had. In these times, I know the only person I can truly change is myself, and the only person who can truly change my situation is me. In the end, the research, therapy and recovery work I've done and the information and insights I've discovered have "saved" my life, even though it cannot stop the "stuff" from happening.

I hope by sharing what I have learned, others – whether a parent, friend, sibling, spouse or child – will find the tools they need to live *their* lives. I share this information because I wish I had known it, that it had been openly and freely talked about, long before I'd spent decades grappling with my loved ones' drinking. This book is by no means exhaustive, and I've purposefully tried to keep it very short and simple. I know, myself, that when I first started looking for information, I was overwhelmed with the variety and depth of the books and research on what I was striving to understand – excessive drinking (alcohol abuse), alcoholism, co-addictions, adult children of alcoholics, codependency, dual diagnosis, how to help the alcoholic stop drinking, how to heal the family, how to talk to your children, family in recovery – and the list went on and on.

At the time, I just wanted something very basic to read that could help me grasp the overall picture. What I've attempted to do in this book is help you reach this same broader understanding (in far fewer pages) because no matter how much you love someone whose

---

[1] Al-Anon is the 12-step program for people who love someone who has a problem with alcohol.

drinking is affecting your life, nor how much they love you back, love will not and cannot make them stop. But the good news is that it's possible for you to truly enjoy your life regardless. For today, I can honestly say I've never been happier, more fulfilled and more at peace with myself. It may not seem like it now, but I promise you things can and will change...I invite you to keep reading because life – your life – really can be better.

CHAPTER 2

You're Not Crazy,
Something Really *Is* Wrong

When Alex finally entered a treatment program for alcoholism, I experienced a giddy – "I knew it, I knew it! I'm not crazy" – kind of a feeling. Finally, he was admitting what I'd been trying to get him to acknowledge all along, namely he really *could not* control his drinking. So why had I put up with it if it bothered me so much?

The short answer, "I deeply, deeply loved him."

The longer answer, "He refused to admit he could not control his drinking." And, because I loved him, I refused to admit it, as well. Instead, I set out to prove he wasn't an alcoholic because alcoholics were people who lost their families, their homes or their jobs because of their drinking. Alex still functioned very well. He went to work, exercised, joined us on vacations, made me feel loved and appreciated much of the time and had many periods of being a truly great person. And, I loved him – that deep, down, in your heart and soul, "love will conquer all" brand of love. So, I spent years trying to convince myself he could get control of his drinking – somehow.

You're Not Alone

Fifty-three percent of American men and women report one or more of their close relatives has a problem with drinking.[1]

Approximately nineteen million American children are exposed to familial alcoholism, alcohol abuse or both sometime before age 18 – that's one in four children. [2]

---

[1] NIH Publication No. 96-4153,"*Alcoholism, Getting the Facts*," U.S. Department of Health and Human Services, National Institutes of Health, National Institute on Alcohol Abuse and Alcoholism (NIAAA), Revised 2004.

[2] "The People Hurt Most By Alcohol Don't Even Drink," The Legacy Foundation, 2007, <http://www.thechildrensplaceprogram.org/statistical_data.php> Their source: *American Journal of Public Health*, January 2000, National Association for Children of Alcoholics.

Complicating it for me was the fact I'd spent decades rationalizing my loved ones' drinking habits as being excessive and causing problems but certainly not alcoholic. That's because I thought a person's drinking had to be either "normal" or "alcoholic." I didn't understand there is another stage of drinking that is excessive and that excessive drinking for a period of time is always a precursor to alcoholism.[II] Since I was not about to label my loved ones as alcoholics, I tried to make their drinking normal, in spite of the problems it caused. Why? Because I was conditioned, like most of us, to believe that being an alcoholic was "bad." It was a sign of "weakness," "a lack of willpower" and perhaps most of all, a sign they did not love me enough to stop. And, if they wouldn't stop, what would I do? I couldn't begin to face that question.

So, my "excessively drinking" loved ones and I spent hours and then years and then decades arguing the finer points of their various drinking patterns. Each one denied their drinking was really that bad. And, with each one, I denied to myself it really was out of their control. Instead, I rationalized their behaviors (and mine), saying things to myself like:

- He stopped drinking for two years before, so of course he can control his drinking.

- I drank. Sometimes I drank a lot and partied right along with him, but that doesn't mean I have a drinking problem (*or does it?*)

- It could be worse. At least he's not mean when he drinks.

How "Rational" Can You Be?

(Excerpts from a journal I kept – notice how close the dates are in these entries.)

April 14 *You came home and said you were going to go on a controlled drinking program for the rest of your life – only 4 drinks per day. You said you probably wouldn't do it if it weren't for us...that if you were alone, you would probably go on as you had been, but that we were too important – you had to do it.*

May 21 *You played golf and came home drunk. Insisted [Susan, a 5 year-old] should learn what a tape measure "really" does and how to use it. Ended up in the back yard with her counting dead snails (killed by the snail bait). You were doing the "high five" hand slap with her and hit her so hard, tears sprung to her eyes... blamed me for it because I exclaimed... "Why'd you do that?" You said it hadn't hurt her until I'd said that...You started yelling the usual...said you were leaving... Didn't come home until the next morning after I'd gone to work—never did call. That night, when I got home from work you said, "I'm sorry about last night, I overreacted a bit." I said, "Overreacted???!!!???..." and the fight was on.*

Fueling my rationalizations was the fact I had struggled with eating disorders (one year of anorexia and eleven years of bulimia starting at age 16). I knew the self-loathing, the shame, the fear and the desperation my loved ones felt over breaking the promises they'd made to themselves to stop or cut back. I knew the insanity of wanting and believing each purge was the last, only to find myself crazed in a food binge two hours later, followed by the mental volley of rationalizations that eased my guilt. But, since I had learned to re-eat successfully on my own, I thought people who had problems with drinking could learn to re-drink. [I would later learn I was correct, as long as the person hasn't crossed the line from excessive drinking (alcohol abuse) to addiction (alcohol dependence or alcoholism). But, I'll explain this concept later.]

And so, over the years, my rationalizations morphed, absorbed, blurred and merged until I had simply made the unacceptable acceptable.

With all of that muddled thinking, the information that truly helped me begin to sort out my life was learning there is a difference between alcohol dependence (alcoholism), alcohol use ("normal" drinking) and alcohol abuse (excessive drinking). The following information is not meant to help you try to label your loved one in hopes he or she will then "see the light." Rather, it is provided to better equip you in validating what you likely already know – your loved one really *does* drink too much and their drinking really *is* the cause of a lot of problems for you and for them.

What Is Normal Drinking?

Sometimes it is easier to get a sense of what is abnormal by understanding what is considered "normal." In the case of alcohol consumption, "normal" is the definition of moderate drinking (a.k.a. alcohol use) or drinking levels that are not likely to cause alcohol-related problems.

Two of the predominant definitions come from the U.S. Department of Agriculture (USDA), as part of its Dietary Guidelines, and from the U.S. Department of Health and Human Services' National Institute on Alcohol Abuse and Alcoholism (NIAAA), as part of its "Clinician's Guide to Helping Patients Who Drink Too Much."

The USDA Dietary Guidelines define moderate drinking as:

- no more than two drinks per day for men, and
- no more than one drink per day for women.[iii]

The NIAAA Clinician's Guide defines drinking levels that are not likely to cause alcohol-related problems as:

- no more than 4 drinks in a day <u>AND</u> no more than 14 drinks in a week for healthy men up to age 65, and

- no more than 3 drinks in a day <u>AND</u> no more than 7 drinks in a week for healthy women up to age 65.[IV]

Note: neither definition supports the idea that a person can "save" their daily drink allotments and then consume them all at once (for example, 5 drinks on Friday night). That's considered binge drinking. Binge drinking is defined as drinking four or more drinks on the same occasion for women and five or more drinks on the same occasion for men. Binge drinking is considered problem drinking.

About That Drink...

Both the U.S. Departments of Agriculture and of Health and Human Services agree **one drink is defined** as:

- 12 ounces of beer

- 5 ounces of wine

- 1.5 ounces (1 shot) of 80-proof distilled spirits.

The reason for the different quantities is alcohol content. The alcohol content in a 5 oz glass of wine is the same as in a 12-ounce beer, for example.

This means common drinks adults serve and/or consume at bars and restaurants, often contain more than one drink, as follows:

- a margarita = 3 – 4 drinks

- a martini = 2 – 3 drinks

- a scotch on the rocks = 2 – 3 drinks

- a standard 750-ml bottle of table wine = 5 drinks

Additionally, the "proof" of the distilled spirit makes a difference. For example, a shot (1.5 ounces) of rum that is 151 proof is the equivalent of two drinks.

So, why the difference between the two definitions?

The USDA Dietary Guidelines are concerned with calorie intake and the nutrients within those calories, as a part of a healthy diet. Alcohol has calories. Generally, at minimum, there are about 100 calories per alcoholic drink. The USDA's guidelines, therefore, are such that they can "fit" into a person's daily calorie intake without adversely affecting a person's overall health or interfering with their body's ingestion of sufficient nutrients.[v] The NIAAA Clinician's Guide, on the other hand, is concerned with alcohol use / abuse / dependence. The quantity and frequency with which a person drinks affects and determines when a person crosses the line from normal drinking (alcohol use) to excessive drinking (alcohol abuse) to alcohol dependence (alcoholism).[vi]

Both sources agree the following individuals should not drink *any* quantity of alcohol:

- children, adolescents and young adults under age 21
- individuals taking medications that interact with alcohol
- women who are trying to get pregnant or are pregnant or are lactating
- individuals who cannot restrict their alcohol consumption, for example, "those for whom one drink is too much and ten drinks is not enough"
- individuals engaging in activities that require attention, skill or coordination, such as driving a car or operating machinery
- individuals who have health conditions or psychiatric disorders (such as bi-polar disorder or depression) that are worsened by alcohol use.

Why the Difference in Numbers of Drinks For Men and Women?

One of the key reasons for the higher number of drinks for men than for women is body water.

Women's bodies have less water than men's bodies. Alcohol is dispersed in body water. So women (with less body water) become more impaired than men after consuming equivalent amounts of alcohol.

Source: NIAAA, "FAQs for General Public," http://www.niaaa.nih.gov/FAQs/General-English/default.htm#women

Assessing Your Loved One's Alcohol Use

The reason it is useful for *you* to assess your loved one's alcohol use is to help you understand what you and they are up against. It is not so you can make your loved one stop drinking nor help them see the slippery slope they are headed down (although they may be open to the information and to making their own assessment). Rather, assessing helps you understand the difference between alcohol use (normal drinking), excessive drinking (alcohol abuse) and dependence (alcoholism), giving you a solid reference point for your own situation. Even if some of this may seem a bit technical, the hope is by understanding the nature of your loved one's drinking, you can free yourself to do the things you need to do to take care of yourself (and I'll give you ideas on how in later chapters).

The following assessment was developed and evaluated over a period of two decades by the World Health Organization's (WHO) Department of Mental Health and Substance Dependence. It is called AUDIT (the Alcohol Use Disorders Identification Test). It was created primarily for health care practitioners around the world as a simple method of screening for excessive drinking. Other professionals who work with people who seem to have alcohol-related problems also find it useful.[vii]

Circle the answer that best applies to your perception of your loved one's drinking. In other words, the "you" is your loved one. [Don't forget, the "size" of a drink matters.]

1. How often do you have a drink containing alcohol?
   (0) Never
   (1) Monthly or less
   (2) 2 to 4 times a month
   (3) 2 to 3 times a week
   (4) 4 or more times a week

2. How many drinks containing alcohol do you have on a typical day when you are drinking?
   (0) 1 or 2
   (1) 3 or 4
   (2) 5 or 6
   (3) 7, 8, or 9
   (4) 10 or more

3. How often do you have six or more drinks on one occasion [note: this is known as binge drinking, and in the U.S., binge drinking is five or more drinks on one occasion for men and four or more drinks on one occasion for women]?
   (0) Never
   (1) Less than monthly
   (2) Monthly
   (3) Weekly
   (4) Daily or almost daily

4. How often during the last year have you found that you were not able to stop drinking once you had started?
   (0) Never
   (1) Less than monthly
   (2) Monthly
   (3) Weekly
   (4) Daily or almost daily

5. How often during the last year have you failed to do what was normally expected from you because of drinking?

(0) Never

(1) Less than monthly

(2) Monthly

(3) Weekly

(4) Daily or almost daily

6. How often during the last year have you needed a first drink in the morning to get yourself going after a heavy drinking session?

(0) Never

(1) Less than monthly

(2) Monthly

(3) Weekly

(4) Daily or almost daily

7. How often during the last year have you had a feeling of guilt or remorse after drinking?

(0) Never

(1) Less than monthly

(2) Monthly

(3) Weekly

(4) Daily or almost daily

8. How often during the last year have you been unable to remember what happened the night before because you had been drinking?

(0) Never

(1) Less than monthly

(2) Monthly

(3) Weekly

(4) Daily or almost daily

9. Have you or someone else been injured as a result of your drinking?

(0) No

(2) Yes, but not in the last year

(4) Yes, during the last year

10. Has a relative or friend or a doctor or another health worker been concerned about your drinking or suggested you cut down?

(0) No

(2) Yes, but not in the last year

(4) Yes, during the last year

Now, look at the numbers in the ( ) for each answer you've circled and total those numbers. According to AUDIT, total scores between 8 and 19 indicate alcohol abuse (excessive drinking). Total scores 20 and above indicate alcohol dependence (alcoholism).[VIII] A score of 0-7 indicates drinking at moderate levels. This is also known as "normal" drinking or "alcohol use."

CAUTION: The AUDIT goes on to say that in the absence of a trained professional conducting this questionnaire (as he or she knows how to ask the question and interpret the answer or dig more deeply for an accurate answer), these guidelines and scoring must be considered tentative – NOT definitive. Additionally, the AUDIT notes that in an ["official"] evaluation, it matters on which questions points were scored. So it's important to review the entire AUDIT document and not to draw any firm conclusions. (See bibliography for source.)

So Why Assess?

According to the AUDIT,

"…the bulk of harm associated with alcohol occurs among people who are not dependent [but rather engage in excessive drinking (alcohol abuse)].

"…people who are not dependent on alcohol (alcoholics) may stop or reduce their alcohol consumption with appropriate assistance and effort. Once dependence has developed, [however] cessation of alcohol consumption is more difficult and often requires specialized treatment.

"Although not all hazardous [excessive/alcohol abuse] drinkers become dependent, no one develops alcohol dependence [alcoholism] without having engaged for some time in hazardous alcohol use."[IX]

So there you have it. You were right all along – your loved one really can control his or her drinking. Or can they?

What Is the Difference Between Alcoholism and Excessive Drinking (Alcohol Abuse)?

Paraphrased, the American Psychiatric Association's DSM-IV (*The Diagnostic and Statistical Manual – IV*) lists behaviors associated with excessive drinking (alcohol abuse) as follows:

If You Loved Me, You'd Stop!

- repeated drinking bouts that get in the way of relationships at home, work or school or that cause problems (such as repeated absences or poor work performance, neglecting children or family, fights with loved ones about the drinking or drinking behaviors)

- driving a car or riding a bike after drinking too much

- arrests for DUIs or disorderly conduct

- continuing to drink in excess in spite of all the problems it's causing, arguing it's either no big deal or it won't happen again.[x]

It is no wonder most of us confuse alcohol abuse (excessive drinking) with alcoholism (alcohol dependence)!

Alcoholism, on the other hand, is defined as a <u>disease</u> by the National Council on Alcoholism and Drug Dependence (NCADD) and the American Society of Addiction Medicine, among many other organizations, neuroscientists, brain researchers, treatment centers and medical and mental health professionals.[XI] Paraphrased, the American Psychiatric Association's DSM-IV lists the behaviors associated with the characteristics of the disease of alcoholism as follows:

- tolerance (needing more alcohol to get the same "buzz")

- withdrawal symptoms (feeling jumpy, anxious, nauseous or shaky; emotional mood swings; difficulty thinking clearly; depression) and then drinking to avoid the symptoms

- repeatedly drinking more or over a longer period than planned for the occasion (which could be an evening at home, a fishing trip or a wedding, for example)

- repeatedly wanting to cut down how much or limit the number of days a week one drinks and not being successful in holding to desired limits

- obsession with alcohol (instead of just pouring a drink or two, going to great lengths to get it, sneak or cover up how much is being consumed or how bad the hang over is); a need or compulsion to drink

- gradually giving up social, occupational or recreational activities because they don't fit with how much alcohol is being consumed (not wanting to go out with friends who don't join in the excessive drinking or not attending events where alcohol is not served)

- continuing to drink in spite of the above or in spite of physical or psychological problems identified as being caused or made worse by the drinking (such as depression or an ulcer).[XII]

What makes alcoholism so difficult to understand for everyone concerned – including the alcoholic – (in other words, to answer the question, "Why is it different than alcohol abuse?") is the addiction component. As defined by the professionals, addiction is the uncontrollable, compulsive need, pursuit and use of alcohol (or another drug), "even in the face of negative health, social or legal consequences."[XIII] For someone grappling with a loved one whose drinking has crossed the line from alcohol abuse (excessive drinking) to addiction (alcoholism), the next important thing you need to understand is what causes the addiction to alcohol. Again, this understanding is not to help you get your loved one to stop drinking (nor, I might add, is it to minimize the issues and problems related to a loved one's alcohol abuse). Rather recognizing the cause of alcoholism will give you further knowledge that is critical to *your* wellbeing.

(See Appendix A-7 for the complete definition and explanation of the disease of alcoholism and Appendix A-1 for more information resources about the disease of alcoholism and the condition of alcohol abuse.)

CHAPTER 3

When Alcohol "Hijacks" the Brain

When people cross the line from excessive drinking (alcohol abuse) to alcohol dependence (alcoholism), they've changed the very structure and chemical make-up of their brain.[xiv] The result is "a true brain disorder,"[xv] according to neuroscientists and brain researchers. The following discussion will help you better understand what's happened to your loved one's brain if he or she has the disease of alcoholism. Understanding what the alcoholic faces may help you accept the idea that there is nothing you can do to get your loved one to stop drinking.

Thanks to New Imaging Technology...

According to the NIDA (the National Institute on Drug Abuse), [which defines alcohol as a drug], "Brain imaging studies of drug-addicted individuals show physical changes in areas of the brain that are critical to judgment, decision making, learning and memory, and behavior control."

Source: NIDA, March 2007, <http://www.nida.nih.gov/scienceofaddiction/addiction.html>

Basic Brain Facts

MRI (magnetic resonance imaging), DTI (diffusion tensor imaging), PET (positron emission tomography), electrophysiological brain mapping and NMR (nuclear magnetic resonance) are new imaging technologies developed since the 1990s. They have allowed scientists and medical professionals to observe the living, conscious brain's extraordinarily complex communications networks as never before. Previously, researchers could only observe the human brain by dissecting it after someone died. This newfound ability to observe the live, conscious brain is what makes it possible for these professionals to declare alcohol dependence a brain disorder, a disease, an addiction.

As you read the text box, "The 'Three-Brains-in-One' Brain Complex," that follows, it becomes apparent that our brain's complex communications networks are critical to our ability to walk, talk, think, feel pleasure and move.

A communication network requires neurons and neurotransmitters. Neurons are specialized cells designed to receive, process and transmit information to other neurons. They fall into three general categories: *motor neurons* (for conveying motor information, like walking), *sensory neurons* (for conveying sensory information, such as touching) and *interneurons* (for conveying information between different types of neurons).[xvi] [When discussing the brain, neurons are often referred to as "brain cells."]

Neurotransmitters are chemical messengers that carry the information between neurons across a small gap, called a synapse.[xvii] There are millions of synapses firing in your brain every second.[xviii]

To start a communications network, "something" – a "cue" – activates a neuron. Cues might include sights, smells, memories or sounds. The activated neuron (the transmitting neuron) sends an electrical signal, which triggers the release of a neurotransmitter (the chemical "messenger"). This neurotransmitter then crosses the synapse (the gap between the neurons) and binds to receptors on the target neuron to complete a communications network.[xix] For an alcoholic (or someone who drinks excessivly), a cue may be the sound of a beer can tab being popped open, the smell of a glass of wine or the face of a timepiece showing it's 5:00 o'clock in the afternoon.

Many of the communications networks in the brain are hardwired. Hardwired means a person does not consciously think about the action that's occurring – it's automatic. Hardwired communications networks occur either by instinct (such as eating when hungry, drinking when thirsty, running when threatened with danger) or by repetitive activation. Examples of communication networks created by repetitive activation include a person's ability to speak a language, type on a computer, ride a bicycle or drive a car, or their adopting a habit, such as nail-biting.

When specific communication networks are frequently activated, those networks become embedded within the brain. When a person stops performing a repetitive activity, the communication networks for that particular activity fall into disuse and may even eventually disappear.[xx] This is where the expression, "use it or lose it," applies to brain cells.

An Example of How Alcohol "Hijacks" the Brain

There are so many communications networks in all three sub-brains affected by alcohol (whether the person is an alcoholic or an alcohol abuser), but for this discussion, the focus is on those in the Limbic System's pleasure/reward center. These networks are commonly

The "Three Brains-in-One" Brain Complex

Medical, psychiatric and scientific professionals actually divide the human brain into three brains or brain sub-systems.

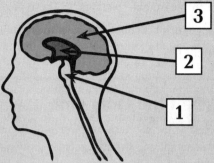

One is the Reptilian Brain (1). Communications networks in the Reptilian Brain control basic functions, such as breathing, heartbeat and motor coordination.

The second is the Mammalian Brain or the Limbic System (2), and it sits above the Reptilian Brain. Communications networks in this brain control our emotions, pleasure/reward/pain center and fight-or-flight system.

The third brain is the Cerebral Cortex (3). It is the largest "brain." Its communications networks control most of our body functions, including our state of consciousness, senses, motor skills, reasoning and language. It is from here that we think and make decisions. The cerebral cortex is often referred to as the executive center of the entire three-brain, brain complex.*

* It is common for other terms to be used to identify these three-brains or brain sub-systems, and there are many sub-components within each "brain," such as the prefrontal cortex within the cerebral cortex and the amygdala within the Limbic System.

Sources: Phelps, [based on the findings of neurologist Paul MacLean], <http://www.psycheducation.org/emotion/triune%20brain.htm>

"Drugs and the Brain," National Institute on Drug Abuse (NIDA) <http://www.drugabuse.gov/scienceofaddiction/brain.html>

called "reward pathways" or "impulse pathways," and they rely, in large part, on the pleasure-producing neurotransmitter, dopamine. These communications networks cause us to experience feelings of pleasure when engaging in survival-type behaviors, such as eating when hungry, drinking when thirsty or having sex. The rewards of pleasurable feelings for these survival-type behaviors are hardwired[xxi] – "designed," if you will – to ensure the human race continues to instinctively do them in order to evolve and survive from one generation to the next.[xxii]

Alcohol affects the same pleasure/reward communication networks as those activated when a person engages in the survival behaviors described above.[XXIII] This is how it works.

When a person drinks alcohol, the alcohol triggers a surge in dopamine levels that in turn triggers a surge in pleasurable feelings.[XXIV] These pleasurable feelings are what motivate a person to want to drink alcohol – in order to reproduce those feelings (and get the "reward" for the activity).

Dopamine Is Not the Only One...

Dopamine is but one of the neurotransmitters in the brain affected by excessive, prolonged alcohol consumption. Others include serotonin, norepinephrine and GABA. [(1)]

GABA (gamma-aminobutyric acid), for example, is the brain's "natural dampening circuit" and acts as a "chemical check on excitatory messages" set off by alcohol and other drugs. It is what chemically "tells" the brain that enough is enough, satisfaction complete.[(2)]

[(1)] Koutlak, Ronald, *Inside the Brain: Revolutionary Discoveries of How the Mind Works*, Andrews McMeel Publishing, p. 118.

[(2)] Lemonick, Michael D. with Alice Park, "The Science of Addiction," *TIME*, July 16, 2007, p. 46.

Used in moderation, alcohol enhances the brain's pleasure/reward communications networks. Used in excess and/or over time, it wrecks havoc with them. How?

Excessive, repeated alcohol use causes rapid surges in dopamine. These rapid, prolonged dopamine surges cause the brain to automatically reduce the amount of dopamine it would normally produce in order to offset the overload.[XXV] This re-balancing act is like turning down the volume dial on a radio when it gets too loud.[XXVI] But then, this reduction in dopamine can leave the person (the brain) wanting more alcohol in order to get that "feel good" feeling again (the one it associates with drinking alcohol); however, for the alcoholic, it has become a feeling the person cannot get because the brain has reduced its normal dopamine production (turned down the radio dial). Not understanding the "mechanics" of what's happening leaves the alcoholic "thinking" it's the lack of enough alcohol that's responsible for the missing pleasurable feelings, so he or she keeps drinking. Instead, it's actually the excessive, repeated use of alcohol that is the cause. Talk about a Catch-22!

This condition – in which the chemistry of the brain goes so out of balance – causes the alcoholic to seek (crave) and use larger quantities of alcohol in order to re-experience

If You Loved Me, You'd Stop!

the dopamine high [something they can't do because the brain has reduced dopamine production] and creates the effect known as tolerance,[xxvii] one of the characteristics of the disease of alcoholism.

Research now shows that, for an alcoholic, the cravings for alcohol can be far stronger than our hardwired drives for food.[xxviii] It's easier to understand, then, just how powerful the craving for alcohol can be for an alcoholic.

The Critically Important "Brake" System

Another critically important component of the brain's complex communication network system with regards to alcohol use is the brain's "shut off" circuitry—its "brakes."[xxix] This is the circuitry that says enough is enough.

Research now suggests non-alcoholics have better "brakes" than alcoholics and that people with weaker "brakes" may have a harder time managing/controlling their cues.[xxx] When cues are not controllable, they become cravings – another component of addiction to alcohol.

Why Successful Treatment of Alcoholism Requires Total Abstinence

Alcohol dependence (alcoholism) cannot be cured, but it can be successfully treated (by the alcoholic, not by you).

If someone is alcohol dependent (an alcoholic), there is absolutely no quantity of alcohol they can drink, EVER, if they want to recover. Not one, not two, not on holidays nor on special occasions, not after ten years of abstinence. **Alcoholics cannot drink** – regardless of what some of the "experts" say or what you may have heard on TV.

Additionally, as long as the alcoholic drinks or thinks he can drink any amount of alcohol in the future, there is no amount of willpower nor good intentions that can help him avoid the next problematic drinking episode. You almost have to think of it as though the alcoholic is allergic to alcohol.

Knowing this can help you to stop the arguments you may be having with your loved one regarding his (or her) drinking habits or believing the promises, such as "I'll only have two drinks a day. No more. I promise." It may also help you stop expecting your alcoholic loved one to behave differently, only to find yourself angry and resentful when they don't. Now you'll understand it's because they can't as long as they drink or think they can drink any amount.

Note: Total abstinence is required to successfully treat *alcoholism*, which is not necessarily the case for treating *alcohol abuse* (excessive drinking). This concept is discussed further in Chapter 4.

Talk About a "Balancing Act!"

Alcohol Also Affects Other Areas of the Brain

Brain imaging technologies and research also show that the addictive use of alcohol shrinks the areas in the cerebral cortex (part of the Cerebrum) that a person needs and uses in order to apply proper judgment and make good decisions.

Take the smell of a glass of wine (the cue) triggering the desire to drink a glass of wine (the behavior), for example. A person whose cerebral cortex has not been compromised by the addictive use of alcohol can smell the wine but make the decision not to drink it.

Alcohol also shrinks areas in the brain stem (part of the Reptilian Brain or Cerebellum), such as those that control coordination and balance.

Source: NIAAA, "Alcohol's Damaging Effects on the Brain," <http://pubs.niaaa.nih.gov/publications/aa63/aa63.htm> AND Volkow, HBO.com/addiction, <http://www.hbo/.com/addiction>.

Biological and Environmental Risk Factors

Scientists and medical and mental health professionals have now identified a number of "biological and environmental risk factors"[xxxi] and symptoms that are also common among those who suffer from an addiction to alcohol (alcoholism) and that contribute to the development of the disease – in other words, these risk factors and symptoms are also found in those who abuse alcohol (excessively drink), and they include:

Social/environmental/familial – 1) the individual's family engaged in heavy drinking at events, gatherings and holidays, or 2) a life-altering event (for example, alcoholism in a parent or sibling, physical or emotional abuse, incest, sexual assault or depression in a parent or sibling) occurred during childhood or adolescence and the individual turned to alcohol to mask the feelings of shame, loneliness, fear, etc., or 3) an individual's peers drank (especially during adolescence or college) and they "joined in," or 4) a parent or sibling abused alcohol during an individual's childhood / adolescence and that set the stage for "acceptable" drinking behaviors,[xxxii] and/or 5) other similar social/environmental/familial situations/events.

Stress – increases the risk for addiction to alcohol in two ways [especially if the social/environmental/familial factors described above are present]: 1) it increases the desire for alcohol to reduce the stressful feelings, and 2) it shuts down the "cause and effect" networks of the "thinking" part of the brain[xxxiii] (the cerebral cortex), which makes rational decisions about how much / when to drink far more difficult.

Early use – as you will read at the end of this chapter, the earlier a person begins drinking (under age 21), the greater their chances of developing an addiction to alcohol.[xxxiv]

Genetic susceptibility or predisposition – yes, research now shows that children with an alcoholic parent are four times more likely to become alcoholics, themselves, than are children without one, and 60 percent of alcoholics have a family history of alcoholism.[xxxv]

Tolerance – most people begin with very little tolerance for alcohol, but for many, frequent use and increased intake over time, increases their tolerance – meaning it takes more and more alcohol for them to feel the same level of intoxication.[xxxvi] For alcoholics, their bodies also physiologically adapt to the increased quantity, which means they'll experience withdrawal symptoms (such as nausea, sweating, shakiness and anxiety) if alcohol use is stopped.[1]

[Appendix A-2 provides more information about the brain and addiction.]

And If Your Loved One Started Drinking Before the Age of 21…

Dr. Kenneth Moritsugu, acting U.S. Surgeon General, stated in May 2007, "Research shows that young people who start drinking before the age of 15 are five times more likely to have alcohol-related problems later in life. New research also indicates that alcohol may harm the developing adolescent brain."[xxxvii] The findings Dr. Moritsugu refers to are similar to those of other organizations, such as the American Medical Association, the National Council on Alcoholism and Drug Dependence (NCADD) and the National Institute on Alcohol Abuse and Alcoholism (NIAAA).

Again, this profoundly disturbing information about underage drinking is made possible by new brain imaging technologies. It is now known the brain is not fully developed before adolescence as previously thought. One area – the prefrontal cortex – is still under development into early adulthood (one's early 20's). This area involves cause-and-effect types of thinking skills. The prefrontal cortex is also developing connections to other parts of the brain, such as the amygdala, which carries "stop" or "hit the brakes" messages,[xxxviii] during this developmental stage. For these reasons, decision-making can be especially problematic for those under age 21.

---

[1] This is why quitting "cold turkey" (not taking another drink) can be physically dangerous to an alcoholic in the advanced stages of his/her disease. It can even result in death. For alcoholics with a high tolerance, it is critical that they go through detoxification under the medical care of a trained professional.

Underage Drinking by the Numbers

According to the AMA's report, "Harmful Consequences of Alcohol Use on the Brains of Children, Adolescents and College Students," [o]*n average, children now try alcohol for the first time at the age of 12, and nearly 20 percent of 12 to 20 year-olds report being binge drinkers (having 4-5 drinks in a row).*

According to the U.S. Surgeon General's March 6, 2007 Call to Action, [t]*he 2005 National Survey on Drug Use and Health estimates there are 11 million underage drinkers in the United States.*

According to the National Research Council Institute of Medicine Committee on Developing a Strategy to Reduce and Prevent Underage Drinking (2004)...*Thirty-one percent of college students met the criteria for a diagnosis of alcohol abuse and 6% for a diagnosis of alcohol dependence in the past 12 months, and more than two of every five students reported at least one symptom of abuse or dependence.*

Because alcohol activates commincations networks (neurotransmitters/neurons) in the pleasure/reward center (inside the Limbic System), the earlier and more frequently the reward center is flooded with alcohol (or drugs), the greater the chances of addiction. [xxxix] Why? Because, in the young brain, neurons that are frequently fired survive, while less frequently fired neurons tend to get "pruned" or die off.[xl] (As stated before, this is the scientific basis for the idea of "use it or lose it.") Further, memory cues involving the use and pleasures of alcohol are also repeatedly reinforced during this critical brain development stage.[xli]

Additionally, teens and those under age 21, whose brains are completing this last stage of brain development, can get drunk on fewer drinks than an adult. Similarly, they can become addicted in a far shorter period of time than an adult. In fact, late adolescence (or the years until the brain is fully matured) is the peak time for developing an addiction to alcohol.[xlii]

All of this medical and scientific brain research should help you understand why a child, brother or sister may already be addicted to alcohol even though they have only been drinking for a relatively short period of time. It will also help all of us appreciate the laws and attempts to reduce underage drinking so as to give our young people's brains the years they need to fully develop and thus reduce the likelihood of lifelong addiction and/or alcohol abuse problems. [See Appendix A-3 for more information about the brain under 21 and alcoholism.]

And now that you have learned a little about how the brain of someone you love can be "hijacked" by alcohol, you should be getting a clearer picture of what you and your family are up against – and, more importantly, that *you* cannot stop them from drinking.

CHAPTER 4

Is There a "Cure?"

All of the fights, all of the arguments and all of the times I screamed at or quietly pleaded with my loved ones to stop or reduce their drinking might have been avoided if I had known this simple fact: when alcohol use becomes an addiction, people drink because they have to drink. It is not a question of willpower, as many assume, because as the new brain research shows, alcoholism is an addiction, a disease. So how does someone's drinking get to the point of being an addiction?

Many factors contribute, not the least of which is ignorance about drinking limits (what's considered "normal" or moderate drinking and what's considered "a" drink) and the risks associated with excessive drinking. Additionally, there is the reality that as a society we still view drinking as either alcoholic or "normal," and we still view alcoholism as caused by a lack of willpower. So we continue to rationalize alcohol abuse (excessive drinking) as normal, for fear that not to is to admit our loved one is an alcoholic (as if abusing alcohol weren't problem enough). For all of these reasons, I found the information contained in this chapter especially helpful when I was starting to sort out my life.

Alcoholics and Excessive Drinkers Are Victims, Too

Alcoholics and excessive drinkers (alcohol abusers) are just as much victims in all of this, as are their family members and friends, because the information about the disease and how it evolves is not openly and honestly discussed in our society. Medical professionals often don't know how to diagnose it nor do they see the red flags indicating alcohol abuse or alcoholism that are there when patients seek help for some "mysterious" ailment or happenstance, such as falling down the stairs, falling asleep during the day or having memory problems. Or when they get their first DUI, friends call it "tough luck," excusing it by saying, "You didn't have that much to drink." Or "Everyone drinks and drives at some time – rotten luck you got caught." So alcohol abusers / alcoholics can't see their drinking as a problem because everyone around them is joining in on the denial since they don't understand or *see* it, either.

A Good Offense is a Great Defense:
Protecting the Drinking – Denial With a Capital "D"

Key to the progression of the disease of alcoholism and the problem of alcohol abuse is denial. Denial is a very human defense mechanism we all use at one time or another to protect ourselves from facing something we just don't want to face. It can be seen in the eyes of a guilty four-year old who denies breaking a vase for fear of being punished, or in the tears of a lover who doesn't want to admit the relationship is over or in the dieter's pretending the size of a piece of birthday cake doesn't really matter.

For alcoholics, however, denial not only distorts reality and hurts other people, it can ultimately lead to death. For alcohol abusers, denial can lead to alcoholism and/or years of destructive behaviors. An alcoholic or alcohol abuser in denial can break a family apart or literally kill another person in a drunk driving accident and still not see their *drinking* as a problem. Unless and until alcoholics or alcohol abusers break through their denial, the consequences of their drinking will continue to spiral downward.

Denial, therefore, is what causes the alcoholic and alcohol abuser to adopt an arsenal of offensive measures in order to protect their ability to drink – everything from flimsy excuses to devious lies, whether they "accidentally" hide a bottle in a gym bag or pretend it's an urgent matter to go out late at night because a "friend" needs help. The old saying, "a good offense is a great defense," is an excellent description of what the alcoholic or alcohol abuser (excessive drinker) does in order to get their loved ones to join with them in the denial that makes their drinking somehow okay. That offense is built on enforcing the two most important "rules" in the alcoholic or alcohol abusing household:

- **Rule #1**: Alcohol use is <u>not</u> the problem.
- **Rule #2**: Do <u>not</u> talk to anyone (not family, not friends) about the drinking nor the behaviors related to the drinking, and, above all, attack, minimize or discredit any family member who does.

These two rules are keys to the "denial of reality,"[XLIII] which allows the disease and/or the abuse to progress unchecked. As the alcoholic's or alcohol abuser's denial-type thinking and destructive drinking behaviors escalate, other, often arbitrary and unpredictable, rules are also adopted and/or changed in order to deal with any cracks in the family's denial.[XLIV] For instance, the alcoholic or abusive drinker may demand the children be in bed by 7 p.m. one evening when they normally go to sleep at 9 or get everyone out of bed to clean up the kitchen when it's never mattered before.

Don't Get Me Wrong...

The alcoholic is still the only person who can decide to stop their drinking. But, they cannot make that decision as long as they drink any amount of alcohol or think they can drink successfully sometime in the future because that's what sets up the denial. This is where the expression, "powerless over alcohol," comes from.

Unlike the alcoholic, the excessive drinker (alcohol abuser) still has the ability to stop or change their alcohol use because they <u>are not, yet</u>, addicted. To change their alcohol use, however they must also stop the denial about "how bad it really is."

The arsenal of offensive behaviors alcoholics and alcohol abusers (excessive drinkers) use to defend their drinking[xlv] include, but are certainly not limited to those listed below. As you read through this list, you may see some that are similar to those exhibited by your loved one. It helps to know that the cause of these behaviors is the disease of alcoholism or the condition of alcohol abuse (excessive drinking). It is not you, their job, your parents, their boss, your children or another family member.

Anger. Alcoholics (and alcohol abusers) are often, but not always, filled with anger – anger with themselves for not being able to control their drinking and anger at others for their attempts to stop them. They use their anger in a variety of ways. It can be out-right yelling or throwing things, it can be sarcasm or mean-spirited "joking," it can be a look or a tone of voice or it can be cutting words said through clenched teeth and a forced smile.

Minimizing. Alcoholics (alcohol abusers) are masters at downplaying or minimizing the significance of what they've done and expecting others to go along with their version, instead. "It was no big deal, everyone was doing shots last night." "For God's sake, why are you nagging me?"

Rationalizing. This is when the alcoholic (alcohol abuser) offers a credible but vague explanation for their drinking behavior – something like, "They served dinner so late. I hadn't eaten all day and the alcohol just went to my head."

Judging. One way to make themselves feel better is to make others out to be less worthy than they are with comments such as, "Well, at least I come home every night." Or "Can you believe how she lets her children dress for school?"

Projecting. Generally, although not always, alcoholics (and alcohol abusers) tend to have low-self esteem (often caused by their inability to control their alcohol use), and they project their feelings about themselves onto others, calling children or a spouse, "stupid," "lazy" or "useless," for example.

Blaming (not taking responsibility for their actions). Alcoholics (and alcohol abusers) often excuse their drinking or destructive behaviors as due to something or someone else – a bad childhood, a bad boss, a no-good friend, an unsympathetic wife, a bad day at the office. [It is important to recognize, however, that some experiences (such as incest or other abuse) can most definitely prompt a person to turn toward alcohol as a "solution." Part of the alcoholic's recovery (or the excessive drinker's ability to change their alcohol use) will involve coming to terms with what happened and adopting alternative, healthier ways of dealing with the feelings, especially those associated with past trauma.]

Lying and deceiving. Alcoholics and alcohol abusers/excessive drinkers must lie, withhold, break promises, cover up and deceive in order to protect their drinking. In time, the lying becomes second nature, and they can lie with absolute ease on so many fronts and act crushed when you don't believe or trust them. They also become very good at deflecting a direct response to your question or accusation with some kind of attack of you. For example, you ask, "Did you stop at the bar on the way home?" and instead of "yes" or "no," they answer, "What is this, 20 questions? And why are the kids still up?"

Is There a Cure for Alcoholism?

The answer is an emphatic, "NO!" However, this disease can be treated. Treatment can be very successful and can lead to complete remission.

To be effective, treatment must deal with <u>BOTH</u> abstaining from drinking *and* addressing the physical, social, psychological and familial issues that accompany the alcoholic's offensive behaviors.[XLVI] This combination of abstinence *plus* the work on underlying issues is referred to as being "in recovery" and is an extremely important concept to understand.

There Is A Difference!

Abstinence = not drinking

Recovery = abstinence combined with an effort to deal with the physical, social and psychological issues underling the offensive behaviors described above

---

If You Loved Me, You'd Stop!

Alcoholics who are in *recovery* tend to be involved in counseling or therapy, possibly taking medications developed for alcohol addiction and/or participating in a 12-step program (such as AA), <u>while</u> they abstain from drinking. [Appendix B offers treatment options frequently used to treat alcoholism.] Alcoholics who attempt sobriety by *abstinence only* are generally not as successful as those who go through "recovery." Those not in recovery are sometimes referred to as "dry drunks"[XLVII] because they generally continue the offensive behaviors they exhibited while drinking though they are not actually consuming any alcohol. The destructive behaviors continue because they are not dealing with their underlying issues (physical, social and/or psychological), nor with their drinking cues and triggers. This, in turn, may also cause them to substitute their drinking alcohol with other equally destructive compulsive behaviors or addictions, such as shopping, Internet porn, cocaine, eating disorders or gambling.

It's important to understand, however, that an alcoholic's recovery program may change over time. What might have been necessary in the beginning (several meetings a day or in a week, for example) may not be necessary as recovery progresses. Above all, the recovery path an alcoholic takes must be left entirely to him (or her) to decide. Just as you could not control their drinking, you will not be able to control their recovery.

The Good News Is The Brain Can Change!

Scientists and medical professionals used to believe the brain was fixed, unchanging and that once there was damage, there was no way to heal the brain. NOW, again thanks to the new brain imaging technologies and research discoveries, scientists and the medical profession are finding that we can, in fact, change our brains. For loved ones struggling with alcoholism and for those who love them, this is huge! Check out Dr. Norman Doidge's research in this area, www.normandoidge.com, as well as Dr. Daniel Amen's, www.amenclinics.com.

Is There a Cure for Alcohol Abuse (Excessive Drinking)?

As for alcohol abuse (excessive drinking) – the "cure" is to stop or change one's alcohol use to levels defined as moderate or normal drinking or to register a score under 8 on the AUDIT (see Chapter 2). It is imperative this be done honestly and forever forward – not the, "I only had two drinks" (when each drink was double or triple the size of a standard drink) or the, "It was a bunch of us from the office – everyone got plastered," or the, "What's the big deal? I only drink a six-pack on Friday and Saturday nights," versions of changing one's alcohol use. It might be helpful for the alcohol abuser (NOT *you*) to seek the advice of a professional trained and practicing in the field of alcohol use/abuse/addiction.

Remember – all alcoholics go through the stage of alcohol abuse (excessive drinking) before their drinking becomes an addiction – the disease of alcoholism. Also, once a person crosses the line from excessive drinking (alcohol abuse) to alcoholism, the person simply cannot drink <u>any</u> alcohol if they are to recover.

Slips and Relapses

For most of us who love an alcoholic, it is our belief that once the person stops drinking, all will be well. Some research now suggests that almost 90 percent of alcoholics slip[1] for brief periods of time.[XLVIII] Other research shows it's not this high. Why does is happen? As previously explained, the alcoholic's brain has been seriously compromised – that is, chemically altered. Memories and cues related to alcohol use have also been deeply embedded, while at the same time, impulse control capabilities have been seriously reduced.[XLIX] Slips do not mean your loved one has "failed" or won't eventually enjoy a healthy recovery.[L] It means healing the brain takes time and effort.

So, why do slips and/or relapses occur? Because, for an alcoholic, it generally takes at least one year for healthy brain functioning to return, according to the National Institute on Alcohol Abuse and Alcoholism (NIAAA). It may even take up to three years. The alcoholic's brain needs time to chemically rebalance. It also takes a while for the alcoholic's brain to develop alternative behavioral responses (new communications networks) to the cues that triggered their compulsion to drink. This means the alcoholic is fighting not only the cues that can lead to drinking but also the chemical imbalance in their brain that has yet to even out (which is where medications can help).

Think of something you might struggle with – say dieting or not exercising. Think of what you go through to counter the struggles with yourself, such as the little voice in your head that says, "Go ahead and eat. It's the holidays. Diet when they're over." Or "It's been a rough day, and you don't feel like exercising; no problem, you were on your feet all day – that's got to count for something." Those internal exchanges mirror some of what the

---

[1] A "slip" refers to taking one drink or drinking for a brief period of time but getting right back into recovery. A "relapse" refers to a return to the alcoholic drinking behavior and denial that was in place prior to abstinence/recovery. More often, however, the terms are used interchangeably.

alcoholic struggles with. However, for the alcoholic, their decision to continue drinking could mean the difference between life and death.

Understanding that the alcoholic's brain takes from one to three years to return to "normal"[2] is hugely important to your wellbeing. It will explain some of the alcoholic's behaviors and help you to adjust your expectations that "all will be well" once they've stopped drinking. It will also help you to tolerate a slip without giving up in despair.

Like Any Other Disease

It is helpful to understand that, like other diseases, treatment for alcoholism depends on the patient's commitment.

Type 2 diabetes, for example, is typically treated with diet, exercise and oral drugs. If a patient forgets to take their drugs or chooses to follow an unhealthy diet or decides to only exercise on Sundays, that person will likely suffer the consequences of Type 2 diabetes. These include damage to the heart, eyes, kidneys and circulatory system. Treating the disease of alcoholism is no different.

Additionally, just as we talk openly about other, more "traditional" diseases, such as Type 2 diabetes, cancer or heart disease, we must start to do the same with alcoholism, in my opinion. No one would choose to be an alcoholic, just as no one would choose to have cancer. Yet, society's continued presumption that alcoholism is caused by a lack of willpower and a complete selfish disregard for loved ones perpetuates the shame and denial that keeps alcoholics from getting the treatment they need. There is an equally negative consequence to family members by this failure to talk openly about this disease.

When you think about it, we don't expect our loved ones to recover from cancer or Type 2 diabetes in anonymity, shrouded in secrecy. Why should recovery from alcoholism or living with someone who abuses alcohol be any different?

Co-Addictions

It is not uncommon for a person addicted to alcohol to be addicted to another drug or compulsive behavior[u] and vice versa. If this is the case, the alcoholic is said to have a "co-addiction." It is also not uncommon for an alcoholic to stop drinking and then become addicted to a different substance or compulsive behavior and vice versa. Co-addictions (or substitute addictions or compulsive behaviors) might include smoking

---

[2] Caution. It takes one to three years for the brain to heal **IF** the alcoholic is both abstaining from drinking and engaging in treatment to stop their offensive behaviors. If they do one without the other, their disease (a powerful physiological, thinking, behavioral and emotional disorder) cannot be fully treated.

marijuana, snorting cocaine, bulimia, anorexia, Internet porn and risky sex, as well as excessive gambling, shopping or exercising.

This idea of co-addiction is important to understand. Spouses and family members are often so grateful their loved one has stopped their cocaine use, for example, that they turn a blind eye when he or she starts drinking alcohol. They convince themselves that drinking is not their loved one's problem (and it very well might not be a problem, *at first*). However, no matter what the addictive substance, according to neuroscientists and brain experts, addictive substances all have "at least one thing in common – *they disrupt the brain's reward pathway*, the route to pleasure."[LII] Additionally, each addiction develops its own communication networks (reward pathways), cues and memories, which means each substance must be treated as a separate addiction. Dealing with the cues and memories that trigger self-destructive behaviors for a sex addict, for example, are different than the cues and memories that set off an alcoholic. [See Appendix A-5 for more information about a few of the addictions that co-occur with alcoholism.]

Dual Diagnosis

A person who has an alcohol addiction and also suffers from an emotional/psychiatric problem (mental health illness) is said to have a dual diagnosis.[3] Research is now showing that "many, if not most, people who are addicted to alcohol or other drugs suffer from another mental health disorder at some point."[LIII] It generally occurs as follows: 1) a person with an untreated minor or major mental health illness starts drinking to self-medicate; or 2) a person's alcohol addiction precedes or worsens an existing mental health illness.[LIV]

Mental health illnesses often co-occurring with alcohol addiction, include:
- ADHD (attention deficit hyperactive disorder)
- bipolar disorder
- conduct disorder
- depression
- post-traumatic stress disorder
- schizophrenia.[LV]

It is critical to understand that <u>both</u> the addiction <u>and</u> the co-occurring mental health illness must be addressed.[LVI] To accurately assess the mental health illness, the drinking of

---

[3] Other terms often used interchangeably with the term, dual-diagnosis, are co-morbidity, concurrent disorders, co-morbid disorders and dual disorder.

alcohol must be stopped. Only then can caregivers determine the proper medication and/or treatment regime needed to successfully treat the mental health illness. Bringing the mental illness under control then helps reduce the compulsion to self-medicate (with alcohol or other substances) and assists with effective treatment of the alcoholism.

If the co-occurring mental health illness is not treated or dealt with, it is less likely the alcoholic will be able to successfully abstain from alcohol.[LVII] Also, the medications an individual takes to treat his/her mental illness are not effective if alcohol is being consumed. However, you must understand that a co-existing mental illness does not cause alcoholism. And, remember, alcohol abuse is always a precursor to alcohol addiction so excessive drinking can also complicate treatment of a mental illness. [See Appendix A-6 for more information about a few of the mental health illnesses that frequently occur in a dual diagnosis with alcoholism.]

A Progressive Disease

Alcoholism only gets worse and cannot go into remission unless the alcoholic stops drinking – *forever*. The progression of the disease generally involves the alcoholic drinking more (often hiding it in the most cunning of places – dog food bag, diaper bag, sports bottles), more erratic, nonsensical and dangerous behaviors and the physical havoc it wrecks on the body getting worse (liver disease, memory loss, falling asleep in the middle of the day, convoluted thinking, difficulty balancing and walking steadily, susceptibility to other diseases). Even if the alcoholic stops drinking for years, "it" eventually picks up where it left off after he starts drinking again. It may take months, but in time, all will be as it was before he stopped. Remember the analogy – "just like riding a bike" – no matter how long ago you rode one, it comes back and soon you're zipping down the road on your bike, with no thought to how you're able to do it. Understanding that alcoholism is a progressive disease will allow you to love your alcoholic and appreciate their good qualities (both past and present) in spite of their behaviors while drinking. It will also help you not to believe that after a period of not drinking, your alcoholic will be able to successfully drink again.

If you love someone who has a problem with drinking, this all might sound terribly overwhelming, even hopeless. Please know your loved one can recover from alcoholism or halt his or her excessive drinking (alcohol abuse) [provided he or she has NOT crossed the line to addiction (alcoholism)] and live a happy, healthy life. If you are feeling at all like I did at this stage, the next question screaming in your head is, "So, now what!?!" The short answer – "Help yourself!" It will likely be impossible for you to believe, right now, that helping yourself is the only way you can help your loved one, but it's true. Likely it's also impossible to believe that you may even need help. That was certainly the case for me – for years and then decades. But I encourage you to continue reading. You may recognize parts of your situation in the remaining chapters, which may prompt you to try something different – for *yourself*.

They'd Stopped Drinking, But Then...

The progression of the disease of alcoholism and its ability to "remember" where it left off is astounding. One of my loved ones stopped drinking for about a year early in our relationship but then started, again. It wasn't long afterwards that his drinking became a problem and the source of many, many heated arguments, broken promises and angst. Several years into the relationship I left him but then agreed to reconcile when he said he'd go on a "controlled drinking program." This program was described in a book. The author claimed that if a person could abstain from drinking for three months and then drink no more than two drinks/day, they really didn't have a problem with alcohol. My loved one stopped for the three months and limited his drinking to just two a day for several months, but in time, the glasses got bigger, and then he stopped counting all together.

Another of my loved ones had stopped drinking for eleven years and actively participated in a recovery program for a number of years prior to our involvement with one another. During the early years of our relationship, he was drinking and it was a problem at times, but I clung to the notion that if he could stop for eleven years, he could get control of it. Within a few years, he had two DUIs.

CHAPTER 5

Now What?

At this point, you may be receptive to the idea that alcohol abuse can be "curable" but alcoholism can not (it's only treatable). You've learned what happens when alcohol "hijacks" the brain of your loved one (Chapter 3). And you may understand that within the brain of an alcoholic, the craving for alcohol can over-ride even the basic human drive for survival – which means there's very little you can do to stand in the way of such a force. [This is especially true if everyone around you is denying the problem even exists!]

All of this new-found knowledge, however, can leave you with one big question: Now what? Do you keep putting up with your loved one's drinking and lies? Do you work harder than ever to keep everything together now that you understand what's going on? Do you pack your bags and leave? What *are* your choices?

In some situations, families are able to break through the wall of denial and actually confront their alcoholic or alcohol abusing loved one about the high cost everyone is paying for their drinking. Some families (and sometimes employers) set up a meeting for an alcoholic called an "intervention." [See Appendix B for a further explanation.]

Since I did not participate in an intervention, I cannot really speak to it from experience. Nor did my loved ones "hit bottom," an expression used in treatment circles to describe the point at which an alcoholic may have finally run out of money, friends, family, their home – or illusions – and at long last admit they have a problem controlling their drinking. Instead, I found myself plunged into the world of alcohol and addiction treatment programs because my loved one checked himself into a residential treatment facility to help mitigate the legal consequences of multiple DUIs.

When he started his program, I lived with the mistaken notion that he would get treatment, stop drinking and everything would go back to normal – as if he were just going into surgery for a broken leg and once the cast was off he (and we) would be good as new. Unfortunately, that's not how it works.

But before I make suggestions about how you might answer the question of "Now what?" – let me tell you a little of what I went through. It might help you – whether your loved one is an alcoholic or abuses alcohol (excessively drinks).

The Turning Point for Me

By the time Alex admitted himself into the residential treatment program, I was so angry I could hardly see straight. I looked forward to our weekly family group meetings at the center because those meetings were the first time I got to "tell" Alex what life had been like with him when he'd been drinking. I was able to say what I had to say without his being able to interrupt me, or even more frustrating, to flip the exchange so it was somehow "my fault." Giving a voice to the family members of the alcoholics (and addicts who were also enrolled in the program) was the whole purpose of those meetings.

It was also comforting to hear the stories of other families – stories very similar to my own. And so for weeks, Alex and I gathered with those assigned to our Wednesday night family group session. I ranted and railed and commiserated with the other spouses and parents of the alcoholics / addicts. I told Alex how truly rotten it felt to be manipulated and lied to and what it was like to suffer through one broken promise after another. And, when he'd throw in a "yeah but…" or a "but, you…" at me, a group member or the family therapist would say, "let her speak."

I listened to the children – those brave enough to speak up – and vigorously nodded my head in agreement, for their stories were my children's stories.

But, I soon realized *Alex* wasn't "hearing" me, and that infuriated me even more. He gave lip service to "getting it" (what all he'd put me through), but I'd heard and trusted those kinds of words many times before (it's why we were still so stuck). So, I would look to someone from the treatment team to tell him for me, believing that if they told him, then he'd listen. It was crucial to me for Alex to understand and own what he'd done. But nothing worked and my anger festered.

So you can imagine my reaction when the family therapist suggested *I* get help. "Me? Why me? He's the alcoholic!" I'd argue. She explained that my getting help would not only help me, but it would also help him. While I wanted to help him, I didn't have time, I argued. I was already juggling life "outside" while he was in residential treatment. The last thing I wanted was to have to do one more thing to help him. I'd been doing that for years, I complained.

I continued to resist her gentle suggestions for weeks. Desperate, I finally took her advice and started attending Al-Anon meetings. I doubled my weekly individual counseling sessions with my therapist and forced myself to find time to attend additional family group sessions at the treatment center. And, as a writer and researcher, I buried myself in books, conversations with others in my situation and websites addressing alcoholism, alcohol abuse (excessive drinking) and addiction. It was during this search that I learned the name of *my* "condition" – a condition commonly referred to as "codependency."

It may be hard for you to accept this right now, but I can tell you that coming to grips with codependency gave me back *my* life. And believe me, I completely understand if the very thought of labeling yourself "codependent" makes you want to slam this book shut. I didn't like the word "codependent," either. And know there is no need to label yourself or put yourself down for something called "codependency," especially if you are in the middle of an entanglement with an alcoholic or alcohol abuser; it's how you've survived. At the same time, if you want to unravel that entanglement and take steps to move forward in *your* life, the key information I'm going to give you in the remainder of this book can really help. As you read further, you will understand why.

Why We Don't Figure This Out Sooner

It can take someone who lives with a non-recovering alcoholic or excessive drinker years before they even think they may need outside help, let alone seek it. There are several reasons for this:

- love and the memory of the love and the relationship that was there before the abusive and/or alcoholic drinking took hold
- the belief that the alcoholic can stop drinking if he or she really wants to; not understanding that if someone is drinking alcoholically, they drink because they have to, not because they want to (See Chapter 3)
- the belief that you can somehow make a difference and so you try everything you can to make the difference, which perpetuates the problem because it continues the denial
- the conditioning you may have received if there was alcoholism or alcohol abuse (or some other "dysfunction" – described later in this chapter) in your family of origin (which could be in your parents or your grandparents, aunts or uncles – anyone whose alcoholism or alcohol abuse affected your parent)
- lack of knowledge about alcoholism and alcohol abuse, what constitutes "a" drink and the differences between alcohol use / alcohol abuse / alcoholism
- the gradual, insidious progression of the disease.

What is Codependency?

It would be one thing if alcoholism or alcohol abuse just struck one day, like waking up with the flu, but it doesn't. It ekes and creeps and slowly crawls forward.

In order to accommodate and survive the progression of the alcoholic's disease or a loved one's excessive drinking (alcohol abuse), the people who love him (or her) have had to adapt and change their thinking and behaviors and join in the denial protecting it. In other words, they've had to adopt their own version of denial. Some describe this progression for the codependent as being similar to what occurs when a frog is placed in a pot of water, which is then brought to a slow boil. The frog doesn't jump out of the pot when it reaches the boil because it's adapted to the warming water temperature along the way.

Through all of this adapting and accommodating of the alcoholic's and/or alcohol abuser's drinking behaviors, family members unconsciously collude to make the unacceptable acceptable.[LVIII] Just as the alcoholic or alcohol abuser is focused (dependent) on alcohol, the family members' lives are focused (dependent) on the alcoholic/alcohol abuser – they are "co" "dependent" with the alcoholic/alcohol abuser on his or her addiction to or excessive drinking of alcohol. This is why alcoholism is often referred to as a "family disease"[LIX] and codepentents are often referred to as "enablers." It's also why a codependent's denial-type behaviors are often called "enabling" (enabling the alcoholic/alcohol abuser to continue the denial that protects their drinking).

Compounding the problem for everyone concerned is society's inaccurate view of alcoholism as a problem that results from a shameful lack of willpower. This assumption – which is wrong – drives the alcoholic and his or her loved ones to continue making one Herculean attempt after another to battle the disease in isolation. And it drives the alcohol abuser and his or her loved ones to find ways to excuse the abuse for fear it might be labeled "alcoholism." Additionally, society is even more silent about what life is like for the family and friends who love the alcoholic or alcohol abuser, and presumes that if the individual stops drinking, then all should be well with them, too. This is another gravely destructive assumption. As I've mentioned, I had been living with alcoholics, alcohol abusers and the family disease of alcoholism for decades by the time I finally admitted, "*I* need help!" It wasn't until the course of my recovery work that I finally admitted how many intimate relationships in my life included alcoholics/ alcohol abusers – talk about DENIAL!

Breaking the Cycles

Changing the Conversations: What New Information and Talking Can Do...

Back in the early 1970s, most people smoked cigarettes, drove cars without seatbelts, road bicycles without helmets and hadn't heard of an infant car seat. Yet, new information and talking about it convinced millions of Americans to stop smoking cigarettes and outlaw smoking in public places. New information and talking about it led to the passage of laws to require bike helmets until age 18, seat belts for everyone and car seats for small children.

That's what new information AND talking about it can do. It allows us to change things for the better. It allows us to change the conversations and break the cycles of destructive behavior, instead of passing them on to the next generation.

But where did this idea of codependence come from and what do the experts have to say about it?

Mental Health America (formerly known as the National Mental Health Association[1]), addiction specialists, medical and mental health professionals, government health agencies and thousands of substance abuse treatment centers define codependency as a learned emotional and behavioral condition that can be passed down from one generation to next.[LX]

The original concept of codependency was developed to describe the responses and behaviors a person (spouse, parent or sibling) developed from living with an alcoholic or drug addict. Subsequent study found that people living with a chronically physically or mentally ill person also developed similar kinds of emotional responses and behaviors. Today, the term codependent has been broadened to describe a person who grew up and/or lives in a dysfunctional family.[LXI]

A dysfunctional family is defined as one where one or more of the following underlying problems existed (or exists):

- An addiction [or abusive/excessive use] by a family member to [of] drugs, alcohol, relationships, work, food, sex or gambling.

- The existence of physical, emotional or sexual abuse.

- The presence of a family member suffering from a chronic mental or physical illness.[LXII]

---

[1] Mental Health America was founded in 1909 and "is the country's leading nonprofit organization of mental health and primary care doctors, nurses and professionals, dedicated to helping all people live mentally healthier lives."

Adult Children of Alcoholics (ACAs)

is the term used to describe persons who grew up with an alcoholic parent.

It is important to understand that the **mere presence of one of these underlying problems is not what makes a family dysfunctional**. What makes it dysfunctional is when a family member's confusion, sadness, fear, anger, pain or shame for the underlying problem is ignored, ridiculed, minimized or denied.[LXIII] This is an important distinction to understand.

For when a family does not openly and honestly acknowledge a problem exists, they most certainly don't talk about it or confront it. Sure, they may yell and scream and rant and rave about and around it like I certainly did but not in a way that leads to change. [Chapters 6–8 will give you a better understanding of what is meant by these statements.] This leaves each family member to:

- interpret what they think is going on

- obey, at all costs, the family rules – especially the two primary rules:

   Rule #1 – "Dad's (or Mom's or your sibling's) drinking (or fill in the blank with the name of the problem in your household _____) is not the issue"

   Rule #2 – "do not talk to anyone (not family, not friends) about Dad's (or Mom's or your sibling's) drinking (or fill in the blank with the name of the issue in your household _____), and above all, attack, minimize or discredit any family member who does"

- adopt coping skills to suppress their emotions so they don't spill over and break one of the family rules (which in time multiply and are ever changing)

- assume their needs and wants are not worthy of attention since everyone's focus must be on the needs and demands of the family member who is ill or addicted or abusing drugs or alcohol and that to ask for or expect attention is selfish or petty.

Because there is no open, honest recognition and/or statement of the problem, one family member may try to reason with the alcoholic or alcohol abuser, while another may learn to "read" their behavior in order to assess what's about to happen (how bad is it going to be?). That family member may then modify her own behavior or try to manipulate another's behavior in order to pacify the alcoholic or alcohol abuser or defuse the situation. A third family member may take it upon himself to pick up the pieces and cover up after the alcoholic's or alcohol abuser's drinking binge, while another may try convince their loved one to stop drinking entirely. One may plead, scream, yell, cry or perfect the silent treatment. Another may work as the peacekeeper between the alcoholic/alcohol abuser and the other family members. And, still another may decide it's all too crazy and leave altogether.

You May Have Something in Common

Many alcoholics (and alcohol abusers) are also codependents. They also grew up in a dysfunctional family. Alcoholics who are also codependents often attend both AA and Al-Anon meetings (or engage in other kinds of recovery work, e.g., therapy addressing both issues).

When codependents place other people's health, welfare and safety before their own in this manner, they can lose contact with their own needs, desires and sense of self. This also affects their ability to have a healthy, mutually satisfying relationship with family, friends, bosses, fellow-workers and significant others. In fact, codependents often marry alcoholics or alcohol abusers or become alcoholics/alcohol abusers, themselves. Crazy as it may seem, it's understandable given their inordinately high tolerance for the unacceptable.

Codependency

is also referred to as a "relationship addiction" because those affected often form or maintain relationships that are "one-sided, emotionally destructive and/or abusive."

Source: Mental Health America | www.mentalhealthamerica.net

Depending on the severity of their situation, codependents may also suffer from chronic anxiety, depression and stress-related medical disorders such as lower back pain, ulcers, insomnia, high blood pressure, skin rashes and migraines. Some may even drink too much. To be clear, however, codependency is not a disease. You cannot die of codependency, and the potential for death is one of the components in the definition of a disease. Codependency is (as previously stated) a "learned emotional and behavioral condition that can be passed down from one generation to the next."

Assessing Codependency

When I was first presented with this assessment for codependency at The Sequoia

Center, I scored a whopping 31.5 out of a possible 36. I encourage you to do your own assessment. Just answer each question with your first reaction and write down whether your response is: (Y) yes or (N) no or (S) sometimes. (You'll see how to score your assessment at the end of the list of questions.)

1. Is your attention focused on protecting or pleasing others?

2. Are you highly critical of yourself?

3. Does it upset you when people are critical of you?

4. Are you more aware of how others feel than of how you feel?

5. Do you have difficulty saying, "No," when someone asks for your help (even if saying "yes" causes you to overextend yourself)?

6. Does what others think of you affect how you feel about yourself?

7. Do you keep silent to keep the peace and/or avoid arguments?

8. Is it hard for you to express your feelings when someone hurts your feelings?

9. Do you feel guilty when you stand up for yourself instead of giving in to others?

10. Do you or did you live with someone who abused/was addicted to alcohol or drugs or was chronically ill (physically or mentally)?

11. Do you tend not to express your emotions or reactions spontaneously, instead taking your cues for how to express them from others or the situation?

12. Do you try to solve the problems and relieve the pain of those you love and worry their lives would go downhill without your constant efforts?

13. Do you hold onto relationships that aren't working believing there is something you can or should be doing to make it work?

14. Do you have stress related illnesses (headaches, depression, skin rashes)?

15. Do you work or eat or exercise compulsively?

16. Do you fail to recognize your accomplishments or minimize them when someone else does?

17. Do you fail to give much thought to what you like or where you want to go or what you want to do with your life?

18. Does fear of rejection or criticism affect what you say or do?

19. Do you feel more alive when handling, worrying about and/or doing things for others?

20. Do you take care of others easily yet find it difficult to do something just for yourself?

21. Have you slowly withdrawn from extended family, friends and/or your regular activities over the years?

22. Do you spend a lot of time worrying or anticipating and planning for every possible eventuality of a perceived problem?

23. Do you shut down emotionally when you are in conflict or facing an angry person?

24. Do you often mistrust your own feelings and fret about whether they're acceptable or justified before you express them?

25. Do you try to "read" the words of others in order to determine their "true" feelings instead of taking what they say at face value?

26. Does your life feel chaotic or out of control?

27. Do you feel a need to argue over differences of opinion until the other person sees and/or agrees with your view and feel angry or wrong or sad if they don't?

28. Do you find yourself feeling angry often?

29. Have you lived with someone who belittles or withholds "normal" demonstrations of love and affection?

30. Do you rarely set aside time to do things you want to do, things that are not "productive" or accomplishing something for someone else?

31. Do you have a hard time doing a "good enough" job or do you keep at it until you think it's just about perfect?

32. Do you have trouble asking for help or for what you need, or do you have trouble with even knowing you need help or want something?

33. Do you find yourself trying to do something productive, even juggling several things at once, most of the time?

34. Do you procrastinate?

35. Do you feel humiliation or that you've somehow failed if your child, spouse or significant other makes a mistake or gets into trouble?

36. Are you most comfortable (not necessarily happy, but comfortable) when things are kind of crazy or chaotic or there's lots to do?

Okay. Now's it's time to tally your score. Each "yes" counts as 1 and each "sometimes" counts as ½. If you scored:

1 – 5	you are probably doing just fine
6 – 12	you may be slightly codependent
13 – 22	you probably are codependent
23 – 36	it's really a good thing you're reading this book!

[In case you're still curious about assessing codependency, you may want to try the assessment in Appendix D. Appendix A-4 also provides more information about codependency.]

Codependency Traits Are Not All Bad

If you scored like I did, you're likely having a reaction similar to mine – "So??? What's wrong with being kind, caring, wanting to make things work out for everyone, deferring to others…?" And, the simple answer is, "Nothing."

Codependents are some of the nicest, most empathetic, "give the shirt off their back" kinds of people. And, there's nothing wrong with that. It's just that when these gestures are always outwardly directed – like at your loved one – in an attempt to get them to do something (like cut down or stop drinking, for example) – then your personal satisfaction slowly becomes contingent on your loved one's reaction to your gestures. For example, when your husband does not cut down or stop his drinking or your child doesn't thank you enough for something you've done, you may convince yourself there is something more you can do or you may get angry, sad or feel like a failure or victim – "No matter what I do, it's not good enough."

The objective, now, is to learn how to re-direct some of this caring and concern towards yourself and to let others take care of themselves. You'll find suggestions on how to do this in the remaining chapters. An additional side benefit of following some of these suggestions will be helping your loved ones BECAUSE you are helping yourself. Really. I've had years of practice, now, and listened to the stories of hundreds of codependents. It really does work!

CHAPTER 6

Reclaiming Your Life

What does it mean for a codependent to reclaim his or her life, a.k.a. "to be in 'recovery'?" After all, the codependent has not really done anything "wrong" (at least in society's eyes), unlike the alcoholic, and often the alcohol abuser, whose lying and deceptions may have destroyed a career, a credit rating, or a family. So what does the codependent have to "recover" from?

Fundamentally, for the codependent, "recovery" means they stop or change the coping skills they've adopted in order to support the rules that exist in an alcoholic/alcohol abusing (dysfunctional) family. These coping skills (described later in this chapter) are so ingrained, it's like they've cut a groove into the codependent's brain – they've become "second nature." So, how does the codependent "recover?"

The simplest definition of "recovery" for the codependent is that they: (1) take steps to understand the disease of alcoholism and the condition of alcohol abuse (excessive drinking), (2) identify the coping skills they've adopted in order to live with it and (3) take steps to change the behaviors associated with the coping skills that are destructive to them. [Remember, not ALL codependent traits are bad!].

In previous chapters, you've learned about number 1 and a bit about number 2 – understanding alcoholism and alcohol abuse (excessive drinking) and identifying how you've coped with it. Now it's time to address numbers 2 and 3 in more detail – identifying unhealthy coping skills and how to change them. These are the focus of the rest of this chapter and those still to come and are often the hardest to tackle because you don't see the problem as having anything to do with you. As far as you're concerned, what you've been doing has been done with all best intentions to help the alcoholic or alcohol abuser (excessive drinker) and the other members of your family. So, it can be extremely mind-bending, so to speak, to even consider changing yourself because who else is going to do what you've been doing and do what still needs to be done?

As you go through these remaining chapters, try to keep an open mind. Read them. Let them sink in. Put them aside. Read them again. Take action ONLY when you're ready. This is not about assigning fault or blame. It's about gathering knowledge.

"A Tough Nut to Crack," As the Saying Goes...

As I've stated earlier, I had been living with alcohol abuse and the family disease of alcoholism for several decades by the time I finally sought help. I had a lot to unravel.

One of the hardest things for me was to have patience with myself. By the time I was ready to admit I had a problem, I just wanted it all to be fixed. Done. Let's move on! But there are many good reasons to take it slowly...

Know that every time you change one small part of your behavior, you're changing the bigger picture, too. Most importantly, you're changing *your* life.

And, one more thing, don't get hung up on whether your loved one is an alcoholic vs. an alcohol abuser (see Chapter 2 for definitions). Alcohol *abuse* can wreck just as much havoc in the family and cause family members to also adopt codependent coping skills in order to survive.

What I present here is pulled from the years of my own recovery experience, which included research, writing, talking with hundreds of other codependents, individual therapy and attending Al-Anon meetings and family group sessions. Through it all, I have found a commonality in some of the "ah ha" moments codependents experience as they progress in their respective recoveries. These are the moments when we say, "Oh, my gosh, I get it." Or, "*Now* I understand." Or, "Damn, I wish I'd known that before." Here are some of my favorite "ah ha" discoveries:

– alcoholism is a disease

– alcohol abuse (excessive drinking) involves many of the behaviors (DUIs, arrests, relationship problems) I'd associated with alcoholism and can be just as devastating to the drinker and their loved ones as alcoholism

– alcohol abuse is always a precursor to alcoholism (although not all alcohol abusers become alcoholics)

– alcohol abuse can be curbed, but alcoholism cannot, nor can alcoholism be "cured" – it can only be treated

– codependents have a "brain thing" going on, too

– the condition of codependency is a progressive one that follows the progression of the alcoholic's disease or the alcohol abuser's excessive drinking (either or both can be checked when denial is stopped)

– trying to "help" is really trying to "control"

– if the person you are talking to and arguing with is an alcoholic with a "disease of thinking and behavior,"[LXIV] he or she and cannot "think straight"

– "respond," don't "react"

These and other "ah ha" discoveries are presented, next. Not all will apply to you nor work for everyone. Nor should they. Each person is different and therefore has had different experiences along the way. So, as they say in recovery circles, "Take what you like and leave the rest." And, above all – be patient with yourself.

Codependents Have a "Brain Thing" Going On, Too!

Recall the discussion about "Brain Facts," the section of this book explaining what happens when alcohol "hijacks" the alcoholic's brain? (See Chapter 3) Just as there is a series of chemical reactions taking place in the brain of an alcoholic or abusive drinker, so too is there a compulsive-like process occurring in the codependent's brain. Instead of that process involving dopamine and the pleasure/reward communications networks (as in the alcoholic's brain's Limbic System), the codependent's brain taps into adrenaline (among other hormones and neurotransmitters) and the fight-or-flight communications networks (which are also in the brain's Limbic System).

The fight-or-flight reaction is one of the brain's non-thinking (automatic) responses to cues or memories that spell danger. When activated, we tend to perceive whatever is going on as a possible threat to our survival and move into "attack" mode, completely bypassing the thinking part of our brain.[LXV] If you mistakenly put your hand on a hot burner, for example, you don't think, "Oh, my, it's hot. I better remove my hand." You simply yank it off.

Many of the chronic verbal and physical exchanges that occur with someone who has an alcohol abuse problem or is an actively drinking alcoholic prompt similar fight-or-flight, non-thinking reactions in the codependent. When a drunk person comes raging towards you, calling you names, you react. You may try to get out of the way. You may start yelling. You may leave the house. But, in general, you don't just stand there – thanks to adrenaline and the fight-or-flight communication networks in the Limbic System.

The repeated surges of adrenaline required to keep you safe in a dysfunctional home – always on high alert in order to uphold the family rules – cause your brain to eventually REACT *without* THINKING to hundreds of situations. What might trigger the alcoholic's (or alcohol abuser's) negative behavior one time, for example, doesn't trigger it the next, and eventually, just about anything might trigger it. What worked to keep the children safe or calm or directed last year, no longer works this year. So a new approach is tried and then another and another. This constant high alert level of reactivity eventually becomes a chronic state of hyper-vigilance. This causes the codependent's brain to become comfortable with a heightened level of adrenaline (and other related neurotransmitters and hormones) and angst. That comfort level then becomes "grooved," if you will (because the same communications networks are used over and over again), and allows a codependent to experience the unacceptable as acceptable.

Part of living your life will be learning how to redirect your non-thinking reactions away from the fight-or-flight communications networks in the Limbic System and toward the rational, calm, thinking-and-response communications networks in the Cerebral Cortex. It is from the Cerebral Cortex that you'll be able to change the codependent coping skills you've adopted in order to survive – change them to ones which will allow you to thrive! Suggestions for how to make these changes will be explained in the remaining chapters, but first, the following discussion will give you a better understanding of the coping skills you've likely adopted. Recognizing them will help you identify what it is you may want to change in order to improve the quality of *your* life – regardless of whether or not your loved one stops drinking.

Knowing Where You've Been Sheds Light On Where You May Want to Go

As we've just seen, living in a dysfunctional home (in this case, an alcoholic family or one in which alcohol abuse occurs) forces family members to adopt coping skills in order to counter the offensive behaviors commonly employed by the alcoholic or alcohol abuser (described in Chapter 4). These codependent coping skills fall under the broader categories of not talking, not confronting, not feeling and not trusting.[LXVI] By their very nature, these coping skills give rise to a number of behavioral and emotional characteristics common among codependents, which is why it's important to take a look at them. As you read through these characteristics, please do not feel attacked or judged or somehow wrong or bad if any of them apply. Adopting these kinds of coping skills[XLVII] is normal (and, believe it or not, healthy) when you live with a person who abuses alcohol or is an actively drinking alcoholic – especially when you don't understand the disease or the condition of alcohol abuse – it's how you survive.

Obsessing – over the alcohol abuser's or alcoholic's drinking and going to great lengths to prevent or stop it, such as searching the house for hidden stashes of liquor and removing them when found, pouring drinks down the drain, listening for the sound of opening beer cans. In time, obsessing over what everyone else in the family is doing or not doing, as well.

All Three Conversations at Once!

Codependents often develop the honed skill of being able to track three or more conversations while conducting their own with the person in front of them. This comes from their tracking what the alcoholic or alcohol abuser was doing or not doing, as well as what everyone else in the family was doing or not doing in reaction to the drinking and in their reactions to each other – all in one big effort to keep a lid on the situation.

Enabling/Denial – ignoring, denying, rationalizing, minimizing, making excuses for and/ or actively hiding the alcoholic's or alcohol abuser's drinking and drinking behaviors; pretending the problem is not as bad as it really is in order to comply with the family rules. It's important to recognize, however, that the codependent's denial is not so much a result of putting their head in the sand as it is a lack of knowledge about the disease of alcoholism and the condition of alcohol abuse.

Controlling and Manipulating – a compelling need to be in control of the people one cares about, wanting desperately for them to either stop drinking (the alcoholic or alcohol abuser), stay safe and on a better path (the children) or see the situation the same way (drinking is not *really* the problem; everything will be fine if we just obey the "rules"). Methods of controlling include little white lies and omissions, deceiving, and/or manipulating. Methods of manipulating include nagging, pleading, crying, criticizing and/or offering constant suggestions in the attempt to get others to do what the codependent thinks is best – all designed to avoid an outright request, fearing a clear, truthful statement might trigger a tirade or drinking binge or break a family rule. Often the codependent believes what he or she is doing is not controlling; it's just "helping," just making sure everyone is getting or doing what's best for them, which often leads to **defensiveness**. This defensiveness stems from the constant fear or worry that others don't understand or agree with them. So the codependent tries to explain, defend or argue until others do understand or agree (which they often don't) and that lack of understanding/agreement then increases a codependent's defensiveness. It's a vicious cycle. Codependents usually can't handle any questioning or criticism because, to them, it feels like a personal attack on their motives, objectives or plans, which in their opinion are all meant to keep *everyone* happy.

Inability to Know What They Feel or Want – difficulty identifying and expressing their own feelings as they spend so much time trying to anticipate and accommodate those of the alcoholic/alcohol abuser and the other codependents in the family. This evolves into caring deeply about what others think of them and believing that if others don't approve, then they must be wrong or bad (because that's how it works under the family rules). Often, this results in their basing their words and actions on their fear of what they think another's feelings or reactions might be or freezing up when yelled at or barraged with another person's emotional outburst (and then physically or mentally retreating from the situation).

The Dance

I'd told my loved one of my fears about what might happen if he insisted on coming home (once his time in rehab ended) instead of following the treatment center's recommendation and going to one of their SLEs (sober living environments). Yet, there he was doing that "thing" he did and me doing that "thing" I did. He with that "I'm so sorry" expression, pressing me to let him come to our home instead of a treatment center SLE, to let him do what *he* wanted – playing on the notion that if I loved him, I would. And there *I* was acting on my feeling that I needed to somehow make it okay for him because if I loved him, I should. After all, he'd stopped drinking, gone into rehab – what more could I want or expect him to do?

It was *us* doing the "dance" we'd done a thousand times before. That day, I was furious to find myself even considering doing it, again. I erupted!

I erupted from a place so deep – a place where years of broken promises, lies, disappointments and deceit had festered, until this one. . .more. . .*tiny*. . .little request proved to be the last straw. I erupted because I simply didn't know how to feel, let alone say, "No, this isn't right for me. I don't care if it's right for you or the man in the moon. It isn't right for me!

Instead, I was getting it all mixed up in my love for him and my ingrained belief that I had to do what *he* wanted as a demonstration of that love. I was getting it all mixed up in my belief that not doing so would be selfish on my part and in my world, being selfish was bad, bad, bad. Suddenly, it all came crashing in, and my fury poured out as we engaged one more time in the dance of manipulation we both did so well – a dance choreographed by years of fear, anger and love.

Arguing – allowing yourself to be drawn into arguments, often over minute and insignificant points, believing that to forgo the point is to admit the other person is right and believing that if the other person is right, then you are wrong. This stems from the constant arguments with the alcohol abuser or alcoholic about what constitutes "normal" drinking, broken promises and the like and always being wrong because he or she is adamant they're not the problem – you are or something else is.

Worrying – about everything – finances, the excessive drinker's or alcoholic's job, the children, what others think, what will happen if _____? Or worrying if what you've said or done is not good enough or is wrong and therefore spending inordinate amounts of time trying to make sure others understand what you've done or said and why. The latter makes sense because most of the codependent's efforts to keep things under control don't work, so they assume personal responsibility for those failures, believing somehow it is/was their fault.

Dependent – staying in an unhealthy relationship because they can't get the other person to acknowledge their part in why the relationship doesn't work. They need that person to admit they, too, have a part in why the relationship is unhealthy and believe that person's acknowledgement or approval is necessary before they can leave or end it.

Angry – sometimes feelings of deep-seated rage – caused by the resentments built as a result of the alcoholic's or excessive drinker's repeated lies, deceptions and broken promises and one's own inability to control what's going on. In time, resentments build towards others in the family who may have a better rapport with the alcoholic or excessive drinker (alcohol abuser) and are not supportive of their view of things.

People pleasing – your attention is focused on pleasing or protecting others; feeling deeply wounded and/or becoming anxious when others speak critically of you; feeling responsible for solving the problems and relieving the pain of those you love or care about; more aware of how others feel than how you feel; feeling miserable because of someone else's behavior; great difficulty saying, "No." Again, this stems from trying to keep the peace and obey the dysfunctional/alcoholic/alcohol abuse family rules in order to be accepted by the family and/or keep it intact.

Fear / Inability to Trust – especially of the unknown, given life with an alcoholic/alcohol abuser is fraught with unknowns, inconsistent behaviors, manipulations, lying and deceit. It's like living with a person with multiple personalities which keep splitting again and again and can never be confronted, as that would break the family rules that enforce denial. Each broken promise, lie, deception or manipulation is somehow masked, excused or ignored. This absolutely crushes your ability to trust and that inability subsequently fuels your fear(s) – all of which spills over into everyday life.

There Really Isn't a Score Card

It took a long time for me to understand I didn't need to get other people to agree that I was right or to see our "difference" the way I saw it. I'd spent YEARS of my life arguing, believing I had to win the argument (which meant they said I was right or that they understood my point) in order for my opinion to be right or okay. Being right was critical to my thoughts of myself as a good person.

I am happy to say this is no longer the case. And my gosh, the time I've gained in my life to do other things now that I'm not engaging in arguments (including the imaginary ones I'd hold in my head to practice for the real thing) is amazing!

Deferring – experiencing a sense of guilt when asserting yourself; not giving much thought to your own self-care but always being there to care for others.

Blaming, Shaming or Feeling Like a Victim – believing that all problems stem from the alcoholic's/alcohol abuser's drinking and trying to shame the alcoholic/alcohol abuser for their behaviors in an attempt to get them to stop drinking and then feeling like a victim when they don't.

Now, all of these coping skills are developed for a reason – so you can uphold the alcoholic/alcohol abuse (dysfunctional) family rules – which means that when you focus "over there," you loose track of what's "over here" – *you!*

Learning How YOU Feel

"Tell us 'How do you feel?' and 'What did you do for yourself this week?'" These were the first two questions we all had to answer during "check in" at our family group meetings at the residential treatment center to which Alex admitted himself. At first, I thought it was *really* dumb. I had one feeling – anger – and as for doing something for myself, I didn't have time! I was too busy keeping the home front going while he was in residence at the center. And, before that, I was too busy keeping everyone squared away while I battled his drinking. Besides, doing something for myself sounded – well – selfish.

Our family group's therapist kept at it, however, week after week. She didn't allow answers like, "fine," "good" or "okay," either. Giving an "acceptable" answer was difficult for most of us, and our therapist was often greeted with a look that said, "So what's wrong with "good," "fine" or "okay"?" We'd eventually learn to appreciate that those answers were vague and intentionally evasive, as we began to understand the reason for her effort. Our family therapist was helping us unlearn one of a codependent's primary coping skills – that of "not feeling." This pre-meeting "check-in," as it was called, forced us to think about ourselves, about how *we* felt, not about how someone else felt. In time, we could describe our feelings with words like, "frustrated," "anxious," "betrayed," "used," "stressed" – even, "hopeful," "happy" and "content."

As for, "What did you do for yourself this week?" it could be something like taking a walk, getting a manicure, watching a football game, not reacting to a loved one when he came home drunk. It could be as simple as going for an ice cream with the children. But, initially, most of us couldn't answer this question either. We'd offer reasons, like: "I was swamped at work." "I had to finish my tax return." "I had to take care of my mother-in-law." "My friend's mother was ill, so I had to watch her kids." These all seemed like reasonable reasons, but our family therapist would just nod and say she understood (and you believed her because she really did), and then she'd gently encourage us to try to do something for ourselves the following week.

Believe it or not, eventually we got that, too. Some got so bold as to do something on a daily basis (like exercising) and others actually did something way out of the ordinary, like taking a week-end trip with a friend. Being able to do something "selfish" was hugely satisfying and (dare I say) "Fun!" It was also freeing because we could see that taking the focus off the alcoholic/alcohol abuser or another family member did not cause our world to fall apart. For most of us, it was also the first time, in a long time, we'd thought about what might (or did) make us happy, not what we thought would make someone else happy.

So, I would suggest you try this exercise periodically throughout the day. Ask yourself how you're feeling without answering "good," "fine" or "okay," and then ask yourself what you would like to do for yourself and do it! Learning how you feel and what you want will eventually free you to do it on a more regular basis, and in time, more often than not. (And, what *you* want may be to do something for someone else. That's okay! It's what *you* want to do.)

Stopping the Denial

As has been stated before, denial is necessary in order to support the two key rules in the homes of alcoholics/alcohol abusers (the rules that protect the alcoholic's/alcohol abuser's ability to drink), and it is what causes the codependent(s) to adopt the coping skills described previously in this chapter. Generally, by the time a family starts to deal with their loved one's alcoholism or alcohol abuse, the denial that's in place is pervasive because the abuse/addiction has been going on for so long. We say things to ourselves and to each other, like: "It's not that bad." "He still works." "She only drinks on the week-ends." "She's stopped for two weeks so of course she can control it." "All adults drink." We act like nothing's wrong and jump on anyone who suggests otherwise. But, it's denial that makes it possible for everyone concerned – alcoholic/alcohol abuser and codependents – to continue unacceptable behaviors and view them as acceptable, as normal.

It Could Be Better!

One of the ways we (co-dependents) keep ourselves stuck is by accepting unacceptable behavior and justifying it by telling ourselves, "It could be worse." Then we list all the things that could be worse: "My daughter could have cancer." "I could be paralyzed." "My husband could beat me."

One day, when I was doing one of those "It could be worse" lists, someone stopped me and said, "Yes, but it could be better!" "Wow," I thought, "she's right."

It took a while, but in time, I'd remind myself of that (right after I'd counted my blessings, of course!), and it's made a huge difference. Instead of living in craziness (because it could be worse), I look for ways to make positive changes when I feel someone's behavior or some situation is unacceptable – because, it could be better!

Stopping the denial does not mean you have to confront your loved one in an attempt to get them to agree that he (or she) has a drinking problem. Nor does it mean the alcoholic/ alcohol abuser has to stop drinking before you can stop your denial. Rather, it simply means to stop telling yourself and the other family members that your loved one's drinking or their behaviors while drinking are not an issue. When you talk about any aspect of the situation with one another or with the alcoholic/alcohol abuser (when they have NOT been drinking) in a calm, respectful tone, it allows you and the other family members to risk trusting that what you *are* seeing and experiencing *is*, in fact, real. It allows you to learn how to trust yourself (your gut feeling) and others in a manner that's healthy for you. Stopping the denial is what allows you to come to grips with some of the destructive coping skills you may have adopted.

Don't Let the Label Stop You

As has been discussed, denial also generally exists in the home where alcohol abuse is the problem (as compared to alcoholism). So don't worry about what you call it. If someone's drinking is a problem, talk about it and most importantly, start setting what are called "boundaries" (see suggestions presented in Chapters 7 and 8).

Likely you're ready to stop the denial or at least think about it and what it means. The big question now is, "HOW?"

CHAPTER 7

Reclaiming Your Life, Part II

Imagine carrying on with your plans for the evening even if your husband doesn't show up on time and you suspect he's stopped for a drink? Imagine letting go of an argument you're having with your wife and making a statement along the lines of, "It seems we see this differently," and then walking away and truly NOT caring whether she agrees? This chapter continues with the suggestions presented in Chapter 6, offering additional ways to change the codependent coping skills you may have adopted, so you, too, can make these imagined situations into realities.

How to Respond Instead of React – Changing *Where* You "Think"

As discussed in Chapters 5 and 6, the life of a typical codependent is one of reactivity, of being on high alert or being hyper-vigilant because of the ever-changing landscape of the relationships in the families of an alcoholic or alcohol abuser. Believe it or not – changing *where* you think – moving from "reacting" to "responding" will have a profound impact on your life. Responding allows us to access the thinking part of our brain (the part located in the Cerebral Cortex), and behaviors based on thinking are far more effective than those based on reacting (those which follow the flight-or-fight pathways in the Limbic System).

For example, if your husband comes home drunk, rather than reacting with anger, take a moment and ask yourself, "Has yelling at him ever worked before?" "Wouldn't he be shocked if I just said, 'hello' and told him I'm headed out to the movies?" This kind of thinking process does not eliminate your angry feelings, but it does allow you to *respond* in a manner that works for you. It's a lot easier to do, of course, when you recall that there is <u>nothing</u> you can do or say to get your alcoholic loved one to stop (or in the case of the alcohol abuser/excessive drinker – to modify) their drinking. Those are decisions only they can make and implement.

> **Reacting** = behavior without thinking. Reactions originate in the Limbic System.
>
> **Responding** = behavior preceded by thinking. Responses originate in the Cerebral Cortex.

Consider these suggestions:

1. Stop yourself as soon as you are aware of that surge of anxious, sad, angry or scared feelings.

   - Some codependents wear a rubber band on their wrist, which they immediately snap when those feelings of anxiety arise in order to jar their thinking – to move it from the Limbic System to the Cerebral Cortex.

   - Some use a word like HALT or THINK or STOP or a phrase or slogan. (See Appendix E for suggestions.)

   - Some use Cognitive Restructuring Techniques (see Appendix F).

   - Some use slogans or sayings – taping them on their car dash, bathroom mirror or desk top – as a reminder of an overall behavior they want to change (see Appendix E).

2. Change the dial on self-talk radio. What? Have you ever had these kinds of one-sided conversations with yourself?: "There you go, again." "You're so stupid." "Why'd you say that?" "I should have finished that and would have if I wasn't so disorganized." Now, ask yourself, "Would you ever talk to a friend like that?" Of course not. It is important to stop being so hard on yourself. When you change the channel on self-talk radio, you can begin to see your many great qualities and in time accept that you are a person with feelings who deserves the respect of others, especially of your alcoholic or alcohol abusing loved one.

3. Banish absolutes – all good / all bad, all right / all wrong. Generally people and situations are not all good nor all bad, all right nor all wrong. This is especially important to remember when you love an actively drinking alcoholic or someone who abuses alcohol. Stopping yourself from reacting to your loved one's rotten drinking behaviors and thus reacting to him/her as if ALL of their behaviors are rotten will help you separate their good qualities from their drinking behaviors. When you do, you can love them with your heart and not your head, and accept that at their core, they're good people with a disease or a drinking problem – a disease or condition that's changed

much of their thinking and many of their behaviors. [Note: This is not to say you have to look for or accept the good qualities in everyone. There are some people whose truly rotten qualities make it impossible to live with them. There are some good people with wonderful qualities that are just not a good match for you. And, there are some alcoholics or abusive drinkers whose drinking behaviors are absolutely intolerable.]

Say What You Mean, Mean What You Say

Learning to speak up for yourself – sometimes called "speaking your truth" – produces amazing results (not only with the alcoholic or alcohol abuser, but with the other relationships you share, as well). It is often hard to do, however, or at least takes a lot of practice, given how long we've been accepting the unacceptable.

For example, have you ever answered a question such as, "Do you mind if I go out?" with something like, "Well, okay if you *want* to go."

When you think about it, however, what you're really saying (without saying it out loud) is, "Yes, I *do* mind if you go out." And, if the person asking the question took you at your word and left, you'd likely be mad at them because they didn't guess what you really wanted them to do. They didn't read your mind.

In this example, you likely don't trust that you have the right to ask someone to do something for you. Asking doesn't mean you'll get it, but at least you won't be mad about something that may or may not have happened. For example, if you'd answered the question, with, "I'd really like you to stay with me this evening," that's the truth of how you feel. It then gives the person doing the asking the opportunity to either say, "No problem. I'd love to stay here with you." Or "How about if we spend tomorrow evening together. I really would like to go out tonight." Speaking your truth gives you the opportunity to receive another's honest answer.

By the same token, you could be on the flip side of this exchange – the one being asked the question. In that scenario, you might "hear" the question, "Do you mind if I go out?" as "Please ask me to stay." For listening is the other side of direct communication and speaking your truth. In codependent relationships, the codependent becomes an expert at "hearing" their *own* feelings – the feelings *they* attach to another person's words; feelings that are not necessarily those of the person doing the speaking. In hearing *your* feelings to spoken words, you are reacting to something that may or may not be true. You are reacting to what you *think* is being said and then adjusting your truth and your responses to accommodate your interpretation, instead of simply taking others at their word. Taking people at their word and asking for clarification if you are not sure what they meant leaves any further explanation up to them to provide and not for you to second guess.

You Don't Have to "Take" Offense

This was especially hard for me to grasp, let alone to do. It's the idea that "taking" offense to what someone says or does is entirely up to me; meaning: I can choose to "take" offense and then argue or feel hurt or lash out; OR I can choose to not "take" offense – the choice is entirely mine.

Here's an example. Say you ask your husband for help with the children after school. He responds, "I'm working. Can't you do it!" Instead of getting defensive (taking offense) and saying something nasty, you can simply "detach" (not "take" offense) and say, "No, that's why I'm asking. Since you're busy, I'll ask someone else." In this manner, you've left his issues with him and taken what's yours to deal with – finding someone to help with the kids. In so doing, you haven't gotten yourself all worked up and angry by fighting about whose work or commitment is more important. You've "detached" from the emotions of the situation.

Another example of indirect communication (not speaking your truth), is when something is clearly bothering you – maybe you're slamming cupboards or have a scowl on your face – and someone asks, "What's wrong?" to which you reply, "Nothing." You've lied, and they know it. A better answer is to say, "There is something wrong, but I don't want to talk about it right now. I'll get back to you when I can."

Now you can likely see that your indirect communication exchanges are the result, in part, of the years you've spent molding yourself to the needs of others in order to comply with the family rules that reinforce the alcoholic's or alcohol abuser's drinking. When a person is "forced" to deny the truth on so many fronts in order to survive, they eventually deny *their* truth – what they do/don't want, what they do/don't feel , what's good/not good for them. They become so enmeshed with the others in their life that their sense of self is deeply diminished. Instead, how another feels is how they feel. What another wants is what they want.

Suggestions to Help With Direct Communication

The following suggestions will help with direct communication. By using some of these suggestions, you can begin to unlearn the codependent coping skills of "not talking," "not trusting" and "not feeling:"[LXVIII]

- *Understand that conflict is simply a difference of opinion, and a difference of opinion does not have to mean a fight.* You don't have to agree with my opinion, and I don't have to agree with yours. No one has to be "right." This is extremely hard for codependents to do because they see unresolved conflict as a reflection on them – as if it's proof they are somehow the one at "fault." Therefore, they tend to argue until the other person agrees they are correct. But as time goes on, this need to argue becomes a target for the alcoholic or excessive drinker and others in a codependent's life. [The "target" concept is described later in this chapter.]

- *Realize "No." is a complete sentence.* You don't have to explain yourself unless *you* want to. If pressed to say more, you can say, "No, not now. Please give me some time to think about it." (Remember: Respond, don't React. And, remember, you have a right to choose how and if you wish to respond.)

- *Walk away.* If you don't want to talk at that moment because you don't know what to say or are too upset, and the other person is pressing you to keep going, walk away. You don't have to stay and fight or talk just because the other person insists on it. Instead, say something like, "I'll have to get back to you on that,"

The Right Kind of an Apology Can Make YOU Feel Better

Because we interpret being "wrong" as somehow being bad, it's hard for many of us to say we're sorry. We often say something like, "I'm sorry your feelings got hurt, but I was just trying to help you." Do you see how this kind of an apology makes it the other person's responsibility to "unhurt" his or her own feelings and protect ours at the same time?

A true apology is when we honestly take responsibility for our part and leave the "but" out of it. Listen to this one, instead: "I'm sorry I interrupted your telling me about what you wanted to do this summer and instead jumped in asking how you thought you could possibly work and go to summer school at the same time. That must have made you feel like I didn't trust your judgment or your ability to think it through. I'm really sorry."

Now that's an apology. And, with this kind of an apology you free mind space for yourself, as well. You don't have to keep justifying to yourself in those hamster-wheel-type thought processes about why you said what you said because you were only trying to do what was best for them or nothing you seem to do is good enough or right, so of course you were justified in your response.

Being honest with yourself about your part in the exchange and then sincerely apologizing for your part, will make YOU feel SO much better. The added bonus is the person you've apologized to will feel like you truly understand the nature of your wrong-doing and that you really are sorry for what you did. Often that helps the other person acknowledge their part, if any, and/or trust it's okay to trust you.

and then walk away. This was really hard for me. I viewed "walking away" as "saying" they were right.

- *Take people at their word.* Try not to attach your thoughts and feelings to another person's words. Take their words at face value. If you really are wondering what they meant, then ask them – directly. "It sounds like you are unsure about whether you want me to go out. Am I hearing your question correctly?"

- *Say it only once.* It is so easy to say something to a person and when that person doesn't respond the way we want them to, to then try to use a prodding question or offer a "suggestion," and then a similar, though slightly different suggestion, again, and again, and even a few days later – again. These kinds of efforts are actually attempts to manipulate and/or control another person's thinking so it matches our own. Manipulation is a huge part of "communicating" in the homes of alcoholics/alcoholic abusers because it's impossible to enforce the rules if one person starts telling the truth.

- *Know that NO ONE has to agree with your truth!* Think about it – when there's an accident, there can be several witnesses and each one will see the same accident in a slightly different way. This is how we must think about speaking our truth. If it's our truth, then it's what we feel, we see, we want, we need. We do not have to get the other person's agreement or approval in order to make it true for us.

Conflict vs Argument

A **conflict** is a **difference**. Therefore a conflict is not "bad" because a conflict is simply a difference of opinion.

An **argument** (fight) is a conflict that is not managed effectively. Therefore, a conflict does not have to result in an argument (fight) if it is managed effectively. How? By direct communication. (For more ideas, see "Suggestions to Help With Direct Communication" on the previous pages.)

Tell Me No Lies, by Ellyn Bader, Ph.D., Peter T. Pearson, Ph.D. and Judith D. Schwartz, explores these concepts in depth.

Anticipate Your Own Slips and Relapses, They're Part of Your Recovery

Be neither surprised nor disheartened when you relapse (going full-tilt back to old co-dependant behaviors) or slip (reverting to old behaviors but then catching yourself and correcting right away). In fact, it generally seems to feel and get worse before it gets better[LXIX] because you are trying to reverse, stop or change behaviors you've been engaging in for years. And, if your loved one is in recovery or working to change their alcohol use in the case of an excessive drinker/alcohol abuser, their individual growth and recovery or change will impact you, as well. And, if you have children – suffice it to say it, that adds a whole other dimension. But don't get discouraged. It really is worth the effort. It just takes time.

So, use your slips and relapses as opportunities for learning, not as reasons to beat yourself up. Unlearning years of the repeatedly activated reactionary coping skills and behaviors will take time. Knowing some of the signs[LXX] that a slip or relapse may be lurking can help you take steps to avoid it or minimize its impact. Here are a few:

- Taking on too much. For some codependents, always doing something is how they keep the negative thoughts at bay. However, taking on more than you can physically and emotionally handle can leave you exhausted, which makes clear-headed thinking even more difficult, which makes reacting and NOT responding more likely. For some, taking on too much also leads to procrastination – feeling overwhelmed by so much to do and not knowing where to start so doing nothing or something else, instead.

- White lies and other dishonest behaviors. When you feel the need to cover up or deny your feelings or values by telling yourself, "It's no big deal, it's just a little white lie," it's generally a sign an old, ineffective behavior is re-emerging.

- Argumentativeness/Defensiveness. Picking at others and/or defending yourself for small (in the overall scheme of things) or ridiculous points or behaviors are signs you are not dealing with a bigger, underlying issue.

- Depression. This is not necessarily clinical depression but the sad malaise – "just want to crawl in bed" kind of depression – that often occurs when you are trying to stuff your own feelings or desires in deference to another person's or because what's nagging you is "too big" to think through so it feels better not to think at all.

- Resentments. There is a saying, "An expectation is a resentment under construction." And resentments are poison for a codependent. They keep us stuck in the feeling, whether it be anger, disappointment or feeling sorry for ourselves. To avoid expectations that result in resentments, try to speak your truth – tell the other person what you want or need or are feeling about a given situation. If the other person wants to change or do as you so desire, good for you. If they don't, they won't. But, if you don't tell them, they can't. It's the expectation they will do as we desire (or they'll "just know" what we want because we think they should if they really loved us) that creates the resentment when they don't do what we expected. That, in turn, sets us up to feel sorry for ourselves or to feel like a victim of the circumstances.

- **Other signs** include prolonged gossiping (which means your focus is on someone else's business and not your own), feelings of inordinate anger (likely because you don't know how to cope with the underlying problem) and "yeah, buts" – every time someone (or even you) offers a plausible suggestion to resolve an issue, you say, "Yeah, but…".

When one of these signs happens, STOP yourself and think more about what is really going on. You may want to call someone you trust to talk it through. Just know you don't have to react immediately or continue reacting. As you calm down and take the time to "reason things out," you'll likely figure out what's really going on (and be able to respond effectively).

Getting the Help You Need

I cannot stress enough the importance of getting outside help in order to learn how to stop the denial and some of the other codependent coping skills and behaviors you may have adopted over the years of living with your alcoholic or alcohol abusing loved one. When you keep going round and round with your problems inside your own mind, you keep getting the same answers.

Outside help can take the form of reading a book like this one or talking to a trusted friend, or it may include some therapy or family group meetings or a 12-step program, such as Al-Anon. [Appendix G lists several suggestions.] The reason for "outside" help is that the conversations you've been having (or not) with yourself or others in your family are not working.

Once again, whatever you choose to do to change your situation is what is right for you at that moment in time (and that could be choosing to do absolutely nothing). You don't (and can't) do all of it at once, nor is there any checklist you have to follow in order to "do it right." The entire objective is to make changes that feel reasonable and right to *you*. See how those feel. If they help, keep at them and then move forward with another when *you're* ready.

And, as you incorporate some of the suggestions above that work for you, and as they become your new way of coping with your alcoholic or alcohol abusing loved one, those new coping behaviors will spill over into all of your other interpersonal relationships, as well. They will become your new, grooved "thinking" behaviors (as opposed to your old, grooved "reacting" behaviors). Best of all, they will free you to enjoy *your* life.

CHAPTER 8

Change Your Relationship With Your Loved One – Reclaim Your Life

Would you like to stop being a target when the alcoholic or alcohol abuser in your life starts screaming, criticizing or blaming you for all the family's problems? Do you want to be armed with verbal skills that can help you get past anger and deal with whatever your drinking loved one throws at you?

This chapter will help you tackle these specific questions and more. It will show you how to remove the "bulls-eye" target from your chest so you're no longer vulnerable to attacks, and it will give you tools for *responding* effectively instead of *reacting* ineffectively. The suggestions contained in this chapter expand on the strategies offered in Chapters 6 and 7 and focus on specific techniques for changing how you treat and/or deal with your alcoholic (or alcohol abusing) loved one. As with all of the suggestions at this stage, these are to help *you* on the path toward a more satisfying, fulfilling life – whether your loved one stops drinking or not, whether you continue the relationship or end it.

Just Like Algebra

While this may not seem like a comforting thought (depending how you feel about algebra), consider this:

If $x + y = z$, then changing x or y will change the value of z.

For example, if $x = 6$ and $y = 6$, then $6 + 6 = 12$.

Now, if you change x to 7 and leave y as 6, then z changes to 13 because $7 + 6 = 13$.

In terms of the families of alcoholics/alcohol abusers, if you change x (and you're 'x'), even though nothing changes with 'y' (your alcoholic/alcohol abuser), 'z' (your relationship) still changes. This is not to say it will be as cut and dried as algebra with a single solution answer, but the concept is the same. Change yourself and your relationships will definitely change – including the one you have with you!

Remember Who You Are Talking To So You Don't Take What You Hear Personally

You would not be reading this book if you didn't know the frustration of trying to convince your alcoholic/alcohol abuser that his or her drinking is a problem. You would not be reading this book if you didn't know what it was like to talk to an alcoholic or excessive drinker at night and then find them the next morning with no recollection of what they'd said, let alone agreed to do.

Now that you understand you have been talking to someone who's altered communication networks in his/her brain and thus their ability to "think straight" – especially when drinking – you can understand that you have not been talking to the loved one you know you once knew (the person they were before their addiction to or abuse of alcohol).

Understanding this helps you to not take personally what they say nor how they behave towards you when they've been drinking (and this holds true when they are early in recovery – remember it can take from one to three years for the alcoholic's brain to recover). Like me, you may have believed it was you they were talking to, criticizing, blaming or raging at. Now, you can see it was not you whom they were attacking, nor was it them, cognitively, doing the attacking. It is a person "blinded by alcohol" lashing out inappropriately.

To give yourself a visual picture, consider this example used in recovery groups. Place a bottle of alcohol in front of you. Stare at it. Talk to it. Tell it to do something. Ask it why it's just sitting there. Heck, yell at it. Does the bottle respond the way you want it to? Now, if you were to pour the contents of that same bottle into your loved one, you would have the same kind of control and/or influence over his or her behaviors – None![LXXI] Remember this if nothing else: their abusive drinking, their alcoholism, is not about you. It's about them.

The Three "C's"

There is a helpful saying in treatment circles called, "The 3 C's," and it stands for:

You didn't Cause it (their drinking),

You can't Control it, and

You can't Cure it.

This makes a wonderful mantra to chant when you're tempted to take personally the words or behaviors the alcoholic or alcohol abuser exhibits towards you when he or she has been drinking.

So, the next time the alcoholic or alcohol abuser/excessive drinker in your life tries to talk or blame or engage in any number of negative, demeaning ways towards you while he or she is drinking or is hung over, try to keep your reactivity low. Instead, give yourself the opportunity to be responsive vs. reactive. Walk away, nod politely or use one of your new coping skills instead of wasting your time talking to someone who's drunk or hung over. Just picture the bottle of alcohol and know that is to "whom" you are speaking. This is a part of the notion of being "powerless over alcohol," and thus powerless over the alcoholic or alcohol abuser when he or she drinks.

Getting Rid of the Target

The offensive moves the alcoholic or alcohol abuser uses gives him/her power WHEN YOU REACT to them – when YOU go on the defensive and employ the old, ineffective codependent coping skills you used in the past.

When you react to the alcoholic's or alcohol abuser's anger with anger or to their denial with accusations or to their broken promises with pleading or a tirade about how rotten they are, you give the alcoholic or excessive drinker a target. For when *you* get defensive, *your* reactions and behaviors become their target. In this way, the alcoholic or alcohol abuser doesn't have to take responsibility for what he's done nor wonder what you are thinking nor feel the shame of having let himself (and you) down, one more time. Instead, the alcoholic or alcohol abuser can lay it all on you. He can tell himself things like, "Why bother, nothing I do is good enough?" "Who wouldn't drink if you had someone nagging you all the time?" "And she says I have a problem with anger – ha!"

Here is a visual. Picture yourself as a door. As long as the door is closed, the alcoholic or alcohol abuser has a target – the door – to pound on and slam into. But, if you open the door (and you step aside), there is nothing there for the alcoholic/alcohol abuser to strike at. They're stuck yelling or pounding at the air. YOU are out of the way.

So how are you going to quit being their target (the battered door)? The suggestions already offered in Chapters 6 and 7 give you some tools for this, but here is one of the best pieces of advice I received to get me started in the beginning. I was told to think of my first reaction and then do the exact opposite because my way of "thinking" was what had gotten me so stuck. Doing the exact opposite is about changing your reaction to the cues and memories triggering your automatic (fight-or-flight) responses. [A word of caution here... as you progress in your "recovery," you will want to move away from this kind of polar opposite thinking. But, in the beginning, it helps to dislodge your grooved, reactionary behavior patterns so that you can be open to more effective ways of responding.]

For example, if you normally quietly and stealthily check up to see if your loved one is sneaking a drink so you can catch them in the act and then call them on it – don't. Don't give them the target of your confrontational words, which they can then deflect with lines like: "What? Don't you trust me?" or "Jeez can't a guy have a drink once in a while?" Instead, do the exact opposite. Go for a walk, run an errand, pick weeds.

If you normally read the riot act to your loved one in the morning following a binge – don't. Don't become the target of verbal put-downs such as: "You are such a nag!" or "Who put you in charge?" Instead, do the opposite. Greet your alcoholic loved one with respect and then go about your morning without confronting them at all.

If you normally use the looks-that-could-kill silent treatment to let your loved one know he or she hurt your feelings when drunk last night – don't. Try, instead, to wait until he is sober and then tell him with words, using a respectful, matter-of-fact, tone, your thoughts and feelings. But do not expect to be heard (remember their offensive behaviors). Express yourself for your benefit, not theirs. Let me repeat: express yourself for your benefit. You do not need to be caught up in whether they "hear" you or agree with you – that's the old dance; that's the target you're removing.

Doing the exact opposite of what you would normally do will likely be extremely difficult at first. But just remember, doing it your way hasn't worked either so you might as well give it a try.

Other target behaviors include: lecturing, moralizing, scolding, blaming, threatening, arguing, pouring out drinks, yelling, trying to fix things, losing your temper, manipulating, speaking for them or uttering the words, "If you loved me, you'd stop." You've likely gathered by now – "targets" are those coping skills we've adopted to survive loving and living with an alcoholic/alcohol abuser.

Remember, NOTHING you do can make your alcoholic or alcohol abusing loved one stop drinking. They must do it for themselves. But, if you remove yourself as a target, you give them the opportunity to truly feel the consequences of their own guilt, shame, remorse, frustration and self-loathing. When you remove the target, they are left to come to terms with their own behavior and you don't have to suffer the consequences. Best of all, you're free to do other enjoyable things because you're not wasting your emotional and physical energy in an exchange that will get you nowhere.

[Appendix F is an additional source for these kinds of suggestions, as are the slogans and sayings in Appendix E.]

Setting Boundaries

There is a humorous saying that when codependents have a near death experience, it is not their own life but rather the lives of their loved ones that flashed before their eyes. This is because codependents are generally living everybody else's lives as they don't know how to set boundaries. Instead, their lives become enmeshed with those of others.

To help you better understand this concept, take a moment to think about how much time you spend worrying about your alcoholic (or alcohol abusing) loved one, thinking about what they should or should not do, of what they've promised to do but haven't done and of the various scenarios you've played out in your mind based on what would happen if they did thus and such instead of this and that. Think about how you do this same thing with others in your life, as well – your children, friends or parents. And then think about all the permutations that arose once your loved one(s) actually took an action that was not in line with all of your thinking. Exhausting, isn't it? Now, ask yourself, "Was it worth the emotional and physical time it took from me, from my day?" Sure, it's important to have your thoughts and suggestions and to make them known, but it's equally important to let go of the outcomes.

So, boundaries are the limits we set on ourselves and on others (and not just on the alcoholic or alcohol abuser – it can be with anyone – a boss, child, friend or an in-law).

> **Setting boundaries** is about minding your own business and allowing others to mind theirs. A boundary is the "line" that establishes where you and your business leave off and the other person and their business begins.
>
> And, while I'm talking about **"minding another's business"**...this refers to letting other people (including our children) take care of anything and everything that is within their power to do. It's okay to offer a gentle reminder or a willingness to help, but it is not okay to butt in or manipulate through variations of the same question or nag until they do what you think is best for them. This includes how (or if) they choose recovery [the alcoholic] or how (or if) they choose to change their alcohol use [the alcohol abuser].

Boundaries allow us to take care of ourselves and at the same time, let go of trying to control. They help us to reclaim "I."

Types of boundaries you might set, include:

- not talking about anything important with the alcoholic or alcohol abuser when they are drinking or hung over

- not driving with the alcoholic or alcohol abuser (they're good at hiding how much they've had to drink.)

I Was In the Car When He Got the DUI

I was in the car when my loved one got a DUI. We'd been at a holiday dinner event at a multi-storied club, and I'd watched him like a hawk throughout the evening. I was convinced he'd only had one glass of wine with dinner, so I was okay with the idea of him driving us home after the event.

He went to get our coats, and it was one of those affairs that take forever to say all the good-byes so I didn't register exactly how long he'd been gone. He explained, as he was helping me into my coat, that he'd gone to the bathroom and then ran into a couple of people on the way out as the reason for his delay.

We drove out of the city – which requires several turns, short streets and stoplights – and still nothing registered. Then, we got onto the freeway, and shortly thereafter, I asked him if he was okay. He was having a hard time staying within the lines. Almost immediately after the words left my mouth, the police pulled him over, gave him the 'walk-the-line/touch your nose' test and took him to jail, allowing me to drive myself home.

Later, I learned he'd found a bar elsewhere in the club and had quickly "slammed back" several drinks during the time he was "getting our coats."

- cutting back your volunteer hours in your child's classroom to just one afternoon a week instead of two or three to leave time for you to do something you want to do

- not having alcohol at family get-togethers (if the alcoholic or alcohol abuser does not want to come, that's their decision)

- getting help for yourself

- stepping aside / removing the target

- deciding not to engage in pointless arguments ("No," is a complete sentence)

- starting a regular exercise program, regardless of whose "crisis" erupts as you're getting ready to go – deal with it later

- not visiting an actively drinking alcoholic or excessively drinking parent out of a sense of duty

- not returning a phone call message laden with guilt, such as, "you haven't called me today…where are you?…it must be nice to be so busy…"

- refusing to give any more money to your alcoholic or alcohol abusing teen

- requiring other family members to help with chores, driving, shopping and the like (Really, you don't have to do it all; others really are capable of doing and helping and will be grateful to be given the chance. Often it's guilt over what they're going through that makes us want to make it up to them by "doing it all" so "at least they don't have to do that, too!")

- taking a nap instead of doing one more thing on your list of things to do

- letting the alcoholic or alcohol abuser take FULL responsibility for ALL of the consequences of his or her actions and inaction

- talking with the alcoholic/alcohol abuser about their drinking and how it's affecting you (and the children, if applicable) – talking in a way (honest, non-threatening, non-judgmental, not while they've been drinking, not with an expectation or demand they'll change or stop) that is not designed to necessarily resolve anything, but to at least start calling it like it is.

Hints about setting boundaries:

- you cannot simultaneously set a boundary and take care of another person's feelings (think about this one for a minute…)

- never set a boundary you cannot enforce (If you say, "Drink again, and I'm leaving," for example, you must be prepared to leave, which means having taken the time to figure out things like what you'll take, where you'll go and how you'll leave.) If you keep changing the boundaries you set, the alcoholic/ alcohol abuser will know they can get you to change your mind the next time and that's what leaves you angry and frustrated with yourself. This is not to say don't express your feelings about the situation. It's to help you see that you don't have to have the whole solution in order to say what is on your mind. For example, you might say, "Sometimes my fear that you will drink again overwhelms me." In talking like this, you are not trying to resolve anything; you are just sharing your feelings about a "conflict" instead of setting up an "argument."

Reminders (the "red flags") about when it's likely time to set a boundary:

- when you find yourself wanting to get someone to do something you think they should do, it's likely your way of "focusing over there" to avoid thinking about or addressing what's really bothering you – try to stop yourself and figure it out (and, it may be you do have a good idea that might help that person, in which case you need to just say, "I have a suggestion, would you like to hear it?")

- when you keep making your point in all sorts of different ways, you're likely trying to control – set the boundary, say it once and then stop (don't worry, they hear you, and then you're free to think and do a lot of other things)

- when you are feeling anxious or ashamed or afraid or angry, it's likely time to set a boundary (and the boundary could be just stopping yourself from going further with your reaction until you figure out the real cause or a better response)

- when you are complaining or rehashing the same transgression over and over or you keep repeating the same scenario looking for validation of the "rightness" of your part in it, it's likely time to set a boundary (and quite possibly the boundary may be to apologize for your part")

- when you find yourself feeling defensive or telling "little white lies" to justify your behaviors or thoughts, it's time to remember you don't have to get another's approval for what you think/feel (set the boundary of stopping yourself until you can sort it out and then speak your truth, and if you owe an apology, go back and make one)

- when you find yourself judging or gossiping, you're likely assigning your thoughts and feelings to what someone else has said or done or "focusing over there" as a way of assuring yourself you aren't *that* bad – stop yourself and ask, "Is this my business?" (and if it's a case of assigning your thoughts and feelings to what someone else has said or done, you can go back and clarify what *they* meant and then regroup)

- when you find yourself thinking in polar opposites – all good/all bad – it's likely something has you way out of sorts, but you haven't stopped your thoughts long enough to cull through the muck in order to get at the real issue (the boundary might be to just take some time to think it through).

Take An Alcoholic's Word For It

The following is an anonymous "Open Letter to My Family" written by an alcoholic and distributed by The Sequoia Center:

Don't allow me to lie to you and accept it for the truth – in so doing, you encourage me to lie. The truth may be painful but get at it.

Don't let me outsmart you. This only teaches me to avoid responsibility and to lose respect for you at the same time.

Don't let me exploit you or take advantage of you. In so doing, you become an accomplice to my evasion of responsibility.

Don't lecture me, moralize, scold, praise, blame or argue when I'm drunk or sober. And don't pour out my liquor. You may feel better but the situation will be worse.

Don't accept my promises. This is just my method of postponing pain. And don't keep switching agreements. If an agreement is made, stick to it.

Don't lose your temper with me. It will destroy you and any possibility of helping me.

Don't allow your anxiety for us to compel you to do what I must do for myself.

Don't cover up or abort the consequences of my drinking. It reduces the crisis but perpetuates the illness.

Above all, don't run away from reality as I do. Alcoholism, my illness, gets worse as my use continues. Start now to learn, to understand...

If You Loved Me, You'd Stop!

CHAPTER 9

Taking Care of Business

Worry. Worry. Worry. Oh my gosh, I was wrought with worry, mostly brought on by fear of what would happen if _____ (he didn't pay the mortgage, she stopped at the bar, he got in a wreck driving home, he got drunk at lunch and forgot to pick up the children or she'd die from cirrhosis of the liver…). It felt like endless worry. This chapter offers some suggestions on how to deal with some of these worrisome matters, as well as some of the things you have had to ignore while being overly consumed with the alcoholic's or alcohol abuser's behaviors. When you take charge of these kinds of things [which, by the way, are your business and one way to set boundaries that are good for your peace of mind], you feel more in control and therefore less anxious. That, of course, is important to *living* YOUR life.

Helping Your Children

Often, we assume that because our children have friends, play sports, get along with their teachers, have decent grades and/or work, then all is well with them. But, growing up in an alcoholic, alcohol abuse or other dysfunctional-type home affects *all* of the members of the family.

The first step in helping your children is to have an open, honest discussion with them about what has been going on and what you are doing to make things better for yourself and for them. This will require an age-appropriate description of alcoholism and/or alcohol abuse. If talking about alcoholism, it will require a very clear message that alcoholism is a disease your loved one will always have, but it is a disease that can be treated by not drinking alcohol and by getting help (treatment). If talking about alcohol abuse, it will require a very clear message that the only "cure" is for the alcohol abuser to change his or her alcohol use. You will want to help your children understand that the disease or condition (not the child) makes the alcoholic / alcohol abusing loved one say and do things that are unsettling or scary or weird. You want them to understand that absolutely NOTHING they've done has caused their parent's drinking problems – <u>nothing</u> – not their fighting, not their bad attitude, not their poor grades, not their messy room. And you will also want to help your children understand codependency and that many of your own codependent behaviors may have been unsettling or scary or weird because you hadn't understood alcoholism/alcohol abuse and how it affects everyone in the family, yourself included. You may have to talk with them about codependent behaviors that they, too, may have adopted in order to cope with the drinking behaviors and your reactions to them.

Unleashed on Innocents

Often we take our fury towards the alcoholic (or person abusing alcohol) out on our children. We may snap at our children or rush them through their bedtime routine or yell at them to stop "making noise" – all activities that might have been fine with us just the day before.

As you learn to recognize you're furious with the alcoholic/alcohol abuser, not your children, you can sit down with them and say, "I'm sorry I yelled at you. You weren't doing anything wrong. I was mad at Daddy because he was drinking and saying mean things to me last night. I should have talked to Daddy instead of yelling at you because I was so mad at him."

You will be amazed at how this helps your children. You validate what they sense is not making sense. You acknowledge your spouse's drinking is a problem that affects you. You also acknowledge that the way you handled your reaction to your spouse's drinking affected them, and that's not fair, either.

Despite differing ages, most children believe what's happening is because they're not loveable (if you loved me, you'd stop) or that somehow they haven't shown their parent enough love to make them happy. Age-appropriate discussions about this are very important, as well. It might also be helpful to arrange for your children to talk with someone outside the family system, perhaps scheduling a few sessions with a therapist trained and experienced with working with children of alcoholics and alcohol abusers or with a trusted pediatrician and/or steering them toward a program like Alateen. The main thrust is to help your children see it's okay and safe to break the two primary, unspoken family rules. In other words, it's okay to:

#1 – acknowledge and support the fact that alcohol use IS the problem and

#2 – acknowledge and support the fact that you SHOULD talk to anyone you consider safe (family, friends) about the drinking and the behaviors related to the drinking, and, above all, a family member should NEVER be attacked, minimized or discredited for doing so.

Other, more practical things you may want to do to help your children can include:

- Designing a safety plan they can follow should they ever feel threatened by the alcoholic or abusive drinker. This might include you talking to a neighbor and asking for your neighbor's permission to allow your children to go to their house, anytime, day or night, if they feel scared. Arm your children with the neighbor's name and phone number and put it in a place where they can always access it. Take your children with you to the neighbor's house so the three of you can discuss this safety plan and how it might work. Your children must know it is not their responsibility to make it okay for the alcoholic or excessive drinker to drink and treat them badly. Everyone in the family should feel safe and protected.

- No driving with the alcoholic or abusive drinker at anytime. That way your childen don't have to try and determine if Dad or Mom has been drinking. This will require you and your children to work out alternative methods for your children to get to their destinations, as well as ways of saying, "No thank you," to solicitations by the alcoholic or abusive drinker (for example, if Dad asks, "Do you want to go with me to get an ice cream?"). Having said all this, it is still a very touchy issue. For no matter how much explaining and talking with the alcoholic/alcohol abuser you may do, they may not be able to uphold the agreement. And, no matter how much you explain and talk with your children, your children may not be able to uphold the agreement. Acknowledging the difficulty of this dilemma for your children, however, is an important step, as is simply having a discussion about it, even if there is no resolution.

[**Caution** with both of these suggestions. You do not want to portray the alcoholic or alcohol abuser as a bad person – after all, you love him/her and are in a relationship. Rather, you want to remind your children their parent is an alcoholic or abuses alcohol, which means that when their parent drinks, they cannot drive safely or they may behave in ways that are mean or not safe for them.]

Every 31 Minutes...

alcohol-related motor vehicle crashes kill someone in the U.S.

Source: NHTSA 2006 / National Center for Injury Prevention and Control.

- Anchor your child's days with some kind of structure. This might include age-appropriate chores, a bedtime story, breakfast together (since dinner can be iffy if the alcoholic/alcohol abuser is actively drinking), a weekly outing (one they choose) – anything that lets your child feel a sense of consistency – that what is good today will also be good tomorrow. This allows them to begin to "trust," too.

The Difference Between "Parenting" and "Codependency"

One of the most difficult things for me was to grasp the difference between "parenting" and "manipulating" (one of the common codependent behaviors/coping skills) when it came to my children. I desperately wanted to help them avoid my mistakes and to succeed as far as they possibly could in school, in sports and with friends so they would have "all their options open." And, in this desperation, I was unknowingly manipulating them with a vengeance to do what *I* thought they needed to do.

I coached, coaxed, nagged and coddled them constantly, practically tracking their every move, always being there to pick up the slack, making sure they had everything, making sure they completed everything on time, etc., etc., etc. It was all done with the best of intentions, but I robbed them of some wonderful opportunities to make their own mistakes and learn from those mistakes. I never realized that in so doing, my unspoken message was, "Here, let me do _____ because I don't think you can." Fortunately, this was one of the first changes I worked on with my therapist, and thankfully, it seems I was able to change my behaviors in time to have made something of a difference before my daughters left for college. My therapist helped me understand that letting them do for themselves was really giving them back their gut feeling – the voice we all have (or are trying to find, again) that tells us what's right and what's wrong for us. He helped me appreciate they'll make mistakes – likely some big ones – and that's okay. Mistakes guide us to make better decisions next time.

Understand Every Family Member Tells a Different Version of "Life at Home"

In alcoholic families or families where there is alcohol abuse, it is common for family members to have wildly different recollections of their lives in the same household. There is often disagreement about what happened or what's happening, how bad it was or is, who was right and who was wrong. This can cause family members to argue amongst themselves – all vying for one or the other to see it from their perspective and agree with their recollections.

It is important to understand each family member is correct. First of all, each individual sees things from his or her own perspective because of their uniqueness as an individual. Think about a courtroom and how you have two sides telling opposite stories about the "truth" of what happened. Secondly, the number of years and the stage at which those years were spent with the actively drinking alcoholic and/or alcohol abuser will also change a person's perspective. Remember, the disease of alcoholism is progressive so as the alcoholic's disease progresses or as the years of alcohol abuse continue, so do their alcoholic/alcohol abusing behaviors (and so do the codependent's behaviors if they have no understanding of the disease, alcohol abuse and/or recovery). So if the alcoholic/alcohol abuser started his destructive drinking when the children were between the ages of 10 and 18, the 18 year old who goes off to college will likely recall time spent in the home much differently than the 10 year old, who lives with it for another 8 years before she leaves home. The way the children recall their time with the non-drinking parent will differ, as well, for the unhealthy coping skills and behaviors adopted by the codependent also get worse as the family disease or alcohol abuse progresses.

This information is helpful so family members don't get unnecessarily out of sorts with one another when they don't all remember "life at home" the same way.

Cover Your Assets

Know where you and your family stand financially. "Why?" you may ask.

If your alcoholic or alcohol abusing loved one is drinking and driving or spending money on alcohol and whatever else might accompany his/her drinking behaviors, you need to be sure you are not financially exposed or at risk of losing everything. This is crucial. Do not accept the brush off that he or she "handles it at the office" or that asking is proof you don't trust him/her. No matter how much you trust your loved one, remember, you are dealing with someone whose brain has been seriously, chemically altered. They may tell you just about anything to protect their ability to handle the family finances to their advantage.

Having said this, achieving a complete understanding of your family finances will likely be very hard for you to do just by the very nature of being codependent. But it is hugely important to you and your children that you understand and protect your assets. Many of the actions suggested below will require you to talk with the alcoholic/alcohol abuser when he/she has not been drinking. You will likely have to practice (a lot) with a trusted friend or therapist on what you plan to say and how you'll say it. Here are some places to start:

- Savings and checking accounts – be sure your name is on the accounts. Agree neither party may withdraw more than $X amount without the other person's signature. Make sure the signature card at the bank reflects this requirement. And, ask your bank to also lower the limit on ATM (debit) cards so only small amounts can be taken out at any one time.

- Order your credit reports – make sure they are clear and your credit rating is good. Ask a bank employee how to do it or use one of the services available via the Internet that provides all three major credit reporting agency's reports (Experien, TransUnion, Equifax). If you find credit cards you weren't aware of, call the credit card company immediately. (It's not uncommon for an alcoholic/excessive drinker to open a credit card, or checking account for that matter, without your knowledge in order to purchase items they do not want you to know about.) Tell the credit card company you did not authorize your signature and you want to be removed from the account entirely.

* If you have been signing your joint tax returns on the day they are due and not fully understanding what's in them and how the various line-items are calculated, you can and should find out. Insist you be allowed to sit down with the tax preparer, and insist that in the future you do this well in advance of the April 15 due date (or file for an extension, if need be, instead of being rushed).

* Ask your loved one if you have any interests in community property (such as the family home). If so, how is it held? If not, why not? These are hard questions to ask – especially when you love and trust that person – but they are critical to your financial future and security. You just never know what the future holds, and if you are the stay-at-home parent, your retirement, health benefits and financial security is entirely in the alcoholic's or alcohol abuser's hands unless you insist otherwise.

* Think about how you might handle what happens if your loved one gets a DUI (a.k.a. DWI) – who will drive him to and from work if he loses his license? How will you afford the legal fees and the increased car insurance costs?

* Consult an attorney or financial advisor. It is possible to pay an hourly rate to talk with an attorney and/or financial advisor (as opposed to giving them a retainer) about your concerns and what you can legally do about them. Family law attorneys would deal with child-related issues, and trust/estate planning attorneys would deal with estate planning issues, as might a financial advisor. Take some time to consult a library book on the subject [check out amazon. com for book title ideas by subject area] and then make a detailed list of your questions and gather any applicable documents, such as bank statements, before you meet with an attorney or financial advisor.

Need Legal Help?

Nolo.com (www.nolo.com) offers a wide range of information on "how-to's" and legal services (such as wills & estate planning, property & money and family law). They also list contact information for attorneys by specialty and state.

If You Loved Me, You'd Stop!

- Take charge of paying the bills so you know where the money is going. If you do not want to be responsible for paying bills, do insist you see all bank and credit card statements. [Once, I had the experience of opening the door to find my neighbor standing there with a homemade pie and the foreclosure notice that had been taped to the door. I should have insisted on knowing the details about the part of our finances he "handled at the office."]

Taking Charge of Your Children's School and Medical Care

Often an alcoholic or alcohol abusing parent who has been in charge of the children's school / tracking of grades, as well as medical appointments (such as age-required medical check-ups, immunizations, bi-annual dental visits and the like) may have let their follow-through slip as their drinking progresses. It is important for you to gently insert yourself into this custodial role for your children's sake. Don't ask the alcoholic/alcohol abusing parent how things are going, nor should you ask your child (children) as that puts them in the position of "telling" on their other parent. Rather, ask your child's teacher to see report cards, for example. Call the teacher and/or school counselor and schedule a meeting to touch bases. Call the children's doctor's nurse for a status check. It's not that the alcoholic/ alcohol abusing parent wants to neglect these responsibilities. It's that they often cannot help but do so as long as they are drinking. You don't have to explain why you are calling. You are their parent, and you have a right to call.

One other thing to be aware of is it's also highly likely your children have been exposed to some horrific behavior on the part of their alcoholic or alcohol abusing parent – especially if that parent is the one who cares for them after school. He or she may have yelled or raged at or hit your children, threatened them with further discipline if they told anyone, left them unattended and/or drove the car with them in it after (or while) drinking. This may have led your child to withdraw from after-school activities and friendships. Again, the alcoholic/ alcohol abuser would never intentionally do any of this – truly – it's just the consequence of his/her drinking behaviors. Nonetheless, as long as he/she abuses alcohol or drinks alcoholically, you'll need to do double duty to protect and support your children at home and after school, even if you are simultaneously working outside the home. One suggestion is to arrange for another responsible adult or after-school program to help fulfill these roles and state your reasons and actions in a conversation with your loved one when they've not been drinking. Know that you do not have to defend yourself. This is an example of setting a reasonable and much-needed boundary for yourself and your children. And, in setting it, you validate for your children that what they've experienced is not "normal," nor was it anything caused by something they were or were not doing. And, you free them of the worry about what might happen if _____.

Life Insurance / Wills / Who Takes the Children if Something Happens to You

One of my biggest fears was that something might happen to me before my children turned eighteen, graduated from high school and selected a college. Who would be their guardian given whom the courts would legally favor? How would my life insurance proceeds be controlled so they lasted until my daughters graduated from college?

In my case, I added a codicil to my Will that explained the situation and stated my wishes for a guardian. Not that a court would necessarily grant my wishes, but I made them known. The point is, you should have a voice and give your children a voice should you not be there to speak for them. Additionally, I set up a living trust to receive my life insurance policy and then made my children the beneficiaries of my trust, stipulating how I wanted the non-related trustee to disburse funds on their behalf. This way, the money they were to inherit would be used by the trustee to issue checks for expenses directly to whichever entity was charging them in order to avoid their inheritance being misappropriated by a well-meaning but abusively drinking loved one.

These kinds of issues might be something else you'd want to take up with a trusted legal and/or financial advisor.

And, Just One More Thing...

Be patient with yourself. It will take time to unravel the behaviors that were absolutely necessary for you to survive to this point. And, you are to be commended for your courage and strength to stay with it and do everything you did to keep it together. You are not at fault. But now that you understand what happens to you and to your loved one when your loved one drinks too much, you can take actions that will allow you to make changes that work for you.

Don't rush yourself. Don't judge yourself harshly.

You'll make lots of mistakes and sometimes feel like it will never, ever get better.

But, it does. Really. Just do what you can, when you can, because any change, no matter how small, is a step away from the craziness and towards a life that's beyond your wildest dreams!

Acknowledgements

This book would not have been possible without the recovery work I did with Jim Hutt, Ph.D., MFT, and Caroll Fowler, MFT, LMFC. I will be forever grateful to them (and so will my daughters!). I would also like to thank my daughters for their willingness to go another round after my repeated codependent slips and for their courage to do what they needed to do in order to break the cycles of this family disease. I want to thank my editor, Mary Claire Blakeman, for her guidance, encouragement and wise counsel.

I want to thank my brothers for always being there for me; they have never wavered in their love and support and have been my sanity on so many, many occasions. I want to thank my dad and step-mom, who have weathered my ups and downs and have always been there to listen and do whatever it took to get me up and going, again; and my mom and step-dad, who've supported and helped me immeasurably over the years, as well.

I want to thank my friends, some of whom go back to the beginning, who have listened as I ranted and raved about the same kinds of problems, over and over, yet supported me in ways I never imagined. Thank you with all my heart for "then" and for hanging in there as I've changed and we move forward in new, fun, lighter-hearted directions.

I want to thank Stephanie Brown, Ph.D., and the Addictions Institute for all of the early and continued work to study and understand what happens in an alcoholic family and what the codependents can do to take care of themselves and/or what the alcoholic family can do to recover as a whole.

And, I want to thank groups and treatment centers like The Sequoia Center in Redwood City, CA, for doing so much to help the families of the alcoholics – for validating what they've gone through and in so doing, helping them find their pathways out.

About the Author

Lisa Frederiksen is as surprised as anyone to find herself the author of *If You Loved Me, You'd Stop!* and creator of the website, www.breakingthecycles.com, which hosts her new book and blog. This focus on breaking the cycles of family alcoholism, excessive (abusive) drinking, underage drinking, codependency and more seems so out of keeping with the subjects of the numerous articles she has published, as well as her six nonfiction books, including *Women's Work, the Story of Betty Friedan; Women's Rights and Nothing Less, the Story of Elizabeth Cady Stanton* and *Freedom Cannot Rest, Ella Baker and the Civil Rights Movement.* Yet, Lisa's new work is consistent with the focus of her writing, speaking and consulting career. Namely, when Lisa sees a problem, she digs in and researches until she understands it and knows she has the most current information and qualified sources. Then she shares what she's learned through easy-to-understand books, illuminating articles and nationally recognized presentations. That's what she's doing with her decades-long experience of dealing with family alcoholism, alcohol abuse and codependency and her research and recovery work in order to help others in situations similar to hers find a way to break these destructive cycles in their own lives.

Previously, Lisa spent 20 years in executive management positions and earned her Bachelor of Arts degree in Economics from the University of California at Davis. She lives in northern California and looks forward to her daughters' visits now that they are both away in college.

Look for Lisa's upcoming books, *How to Co-Parent When Your Spouse (or Ex) Drinks Too Much* and *What Teens Need to Know When A Family Member Drinks Too Much.*

Visit her website:

www.breakingthecycles.com

for the latest research and information on alcoholism, excessive drinking (alcohol abuse), addiction, underage drinking, co-addictions, dual diagnosis, codependency and more –

and join in the conversations to help break the cycles.

Appendices

Appendix A-1: About the Disease of Alcoholism and the Condition of Excessive Drinking (Alcohol Abuse)

"Alcohol Abuse Diagnosis," Mental Health Channel, <http://www.mentalhealthchannel.net/alcohol/diagnosis.shtml>

"Alcohol and Drug Abuse, Addiction and Co-Occurring Disorders," National Mental Health Association (NMHA), 2007, <http://www1.nmha.org/substance/advocate.cfm>

"AUDIT (The Alcohol Use Disorders Identification Test)," World Health Organization (WHO), Department of Mental Health and Substance Dependence, Second Edition, 2001, <http://whqlibdoc.who.int/hq/2001/WHO_MSD_MSB_01.6a.pdf>

"Definition of Alcoholism," the National Council on Alcoholism and Drug Dependence, NCADD, 1990, <http://www.ncadd.org/facts/defalc.html>

National Institute on Alcohol Abuse and Alcoholism (NIAAA), <http://www.niaaa.nih.gov> Makes available free publications on all aspects of alcohol abuse and alcoholism.

NIH Publication No. 96-4153,"*Alcoholism, Getting the Facts*," U.S. Department of Health and Human Services, National Institutes of Health, National Institute on Alcohol Abuse and Alcoholism (NIAAA), Revised 2004.

"Understanding Addiction," Home Box Office, Inc. (HBO), the Robert Wood Johnson Foundation, the NIAAA and the NIDA (National Institute on Drug Abuse), Home Box Office, Inc.: March 2007, < http://www.hbo.com/addiction/>

U.S. Department of Health & Human Services, National Institutes of Health, National Institute on Alcohol Abuse and Alcoholism (NIAAA)'s 2005, Clinician's Guide, "Helping Patients Who Drink Too Much," visit the NIAAA website link, <http://www.niaaa.nih.gov/Publications/EducationTrainingMaterials/guide.htm>

U.S. Department of Health and Human Services, National Institutes of Health, National Institute on Alcohol Abuse and Alcoholism (NIAAA) website link, "Facts for the General Public," <http://www.niaaa.nih.gov/FAQs/General-English/default.htm>

U.S. Department of Health and Human Services and the U.S. Department of Agriculture (USDA), "Dietary Guidelines for Americans 2005, Chapter 9, 'Alcoholic Beverages,'" USDA/HHS: Updated 2/05/07, <http://www.health.gov/dietaryguidelines/dga2005/document/html/chapter9.htm>

Appendix A-2: About the Brain and Addiction to Alcohol

The Addiction Project," HBO, Inc., in partnership with the Robert Wood Johnson Foundation, National Institute of Drug Abuse (NIDA) and the National Institute on Alcohol Abuse and Alcoholism (NIAAA), March 2007, <www.hbo.com/addiction>

Amen, Daniel G., M.D., "Which Brain Do You Want?" (DVD), The Amen Clinic, 2004, <www.amenclinics.com>

"The Brain From Top to Bottom," Canadian Institutes of Health Research: Institute of Neurosciences, Mental Health and Addiction, <http://thebrain.mcgill.ca/flash/index_a.html>

Stufflebeam, Robert, "Neurons, Synapses, and Neurotransmission: An Introduction," Normal, IL: The Mind / Brain Project, Consortium on Mind/Brain Science Instruction, 2006, <http://www.mind.ilstu.edu/curriculum/neurons_intro/neurons_intro.php>

Appendix A-3: About the Brain Under 21 and Addiction to Alcohol

Aaron White, Ph.D., "Alcohol and the Adolescent Brain," Department of Psychiatry, Duke Medical Center, Durham, SC, 2004, <http://www.duke.edu/~amwhite/Adolescence/index.html#>

AMA's February 2007 report, "Harmful Consequences of Alcohol Use on the Brains of Children, Adolescents and College Students," AMA's website link, <www.ama-assn.org/ama/pub/category/9416.html>

Amen, Daniel G., M.D., "Which Brain Do You Want?" (DVD), The Amen Clinic, 2004, <www.amenclinics.com>

NIAAA's publication, "Alcohol and Development in Youth – A Multidisciplinary Overview,"
Volume 28, Number 3, 2004/2005, NIAAA's website link, <http://pubs.niaaa.nih.gov/publications/arh283/toc28-3.htm>

Rogers, Peter D., Ph.D. and Lea Goldstein, Ph.D., *Drugs and Your Kid: How to Tell if Your Child Has a Drug/Alcohol Problem & What to Do About It*, Oakland, CA: New Harbinger Publications, 2002.

Appendix A-4: About Codependency

Beattie, Melody, *Codependent No More, How to Stop Controlling Others and Start Caring For Yourself*, Center City, MN: Hazelden, 1992.

Black, Claudia, *It Will Never Happen to Me: Growing Up With Addiction as Youngsters, Adolescents, Adults*, Center City, MN: Hazelden, 2nd edition, 2002.

"Codependency," Mental Health America (formerly known as the National Mental Health Association), <www.mentalhealthamerica.net/go/codependency>

"Codependency Fact Sheet," Mental Health America, <www1.nmha.org/infoctr/factsheets/43.cfm>

"Is Your Life Affected By Someone's Drinking?" Al-Anon/Alateen, Al-Anon Family Group
Headquarters,

National Association for Children of Alcoholics, <http://www.recoverymonth.gov/2006/
kit/html/Targeted_Outreach/families.aspx>

Appendix A-5: About Addictions That Frequently Co-occur With Alcoholism

Drugs
National Institute on Drug Abuse • (301) 443-1124 • www.drugabuse.gov

Narcotics Anonymous (NA) • (818) 773-9999 • http://www.na.org/

Food and Eating Disorders
National Eating Disorders Association • (800) 931-2237
http://www.nationaleatingdisorders.org/

Overeaters Anonymous • (505) 891-2664 • www.oa.org

Gambling
National Council on Problem Gambling • (800) 522-4700 • http://www.ncpgambling.org/

Gamblers Anonymous • (213) 386-8789 • http://www.gamblersanonymous.org/

Sex and/or Porn
Sexaholics Anonymous • (866) 424-8777 • http://www.sa.org/

Appendix A-6: About a Few of the Mental Health Illnesses That Frequently Occur in a Dual Diagnosis With Alcoholism

Dual Diagnosis In General
U.S. Department of Health and Human Services' Substance Abuse & Mental
Health Services Administration (SAMHSA)
800-729-6686 • http://www.samhsa.gov/Hottopics/TIP42_interim.aspx

ADHD (Attention Deficit Hyperactive Disorder)
National Institute of Mental Health (NIMH) - ADHD
http://www.nimh.nih.gov/health/publications/adhd/summary.shtml

Medline Plus, a service of the U.S. National Library of Medicine and the
National Institutes of Health - ADHD
http://www.nlm.nih.gov/medlineplus/attentiondeficithyperactivitydisorder.html

Bipolar Disorder
National Institute of Mental Health (NIMH) – Bipolar Disorder
http://www.nimh.nih.gov/health/publications/bipolar-disorder/
complete-publication.shtml

Medline Plus, a service of the U.S. National Library of Medicine and the National Institutes of Health – Bipolar Disorder
http://www.nlm.nih.gov/medlineplus/bipolardisorder.html

Post-traumatic Stress Disorder

National Institute of Mental Health (NIMH) – Post-traumatic Stress Disorder
http://www.nimh.nih.gov/health/publications/
post-traumatic-stress-disorder-a-real-illness/summary.shtml

Medline Plus, a service of the U.S. National Library of Medicine and the National Institutes of Health - Post-traumatic Stress Disorder
http://www.nlm.nih.gov/medlineplus/posttraumaticstressdisorder.html

Schizophrenia

National Institute of Mental Health (NIMH) - Schizophrenia
http://www.nimh.nih.gov/health/publications/schizophrenia/summary.shtml

Medline Plus, a service of the U.S. National Library of Medicine and the National Institutes of Health - Schizophrenia http://www.nlm.nih.gov/
medlineplus/schizophrenia.html

Appendix A-7: Complete Definition and Explanation of the Disease of Alcoholism

*Alcoholism is a **primary**, chronic **disease** with genetic, psychosocial, and environmental factors influencing its development and manifestations. The disease is **often progressive and fatal**. It is characterized by continuous or periodic **impaired control** over drinking, **preoccupation** with alcohol, the use of alcohol despite **adverse consequences**, and distortions in thinking, most notably **denial**.*

The medical definitions of the keywords in **bold** print in the paragraph above are given below (and quoted from the same source) for further clarification:

Primary refers to the nature of alcoholism as a disease entity in addition to and separate from other pathophysiologic states which may be associated with it. 'Primary' suggests that alcoholism, as an addiction, is not a symptom of an underlying disease state.

Disease means an involuntary disability. It represents the sum of the abnormal phenomena displayed by a group of individuals. These phenomena are associated with a specified common set of characteristics by which these individuals differ from the norm, and which places them at a disadvantage.

Often progressive and fatal means that the disease persists over time and that physical, emotional, and social changes are often cumulative and may progress as drinking continues. Alcoholism causes premature death through overdose, organic complications involving the brain, liver, heart and many other organs, and by contributing to suicide, homicide, motor vehicle crashes, and other traumatic events.

Impaired control means the inability to limit alcohol use or to consistently limit on any drinking occasion the duration of the episode, the quantity consumed, and/or the behavioral consequences of drinking.

Preoccupation in association with alcohol use indicates excessive, focused attention given to the drug alcohol, its effects, and/or its use. The relative value thus assigned to alcohol by the individual often leads to a diversion of energies away from important life concerns.

Adverse consequences are alcohol-related problems or impairments in such areas as: physical health (e.g., alcohol withdrawal syndromes, liver disease, gastritis, anemia, neurological disorders); psychological functioning (e.g., impairments in cognition, changes in mood and behavior); interpersonal functioning (e.g., marital problems and child abuse, impaired social relationships); occupational functioning (e.g., scholastic or job problems); and legal, financial, or spiritual problems.

Denial is used here not only in the psychoanalytic sense of a single psychological defense mechanism disavowing the significance of events, but more broadly to include a range of psychological maneuvers designed to reduce awareness of the fact that alcohol use is the cause of an individual's problems rather than a solution to those problems. Denial becomes an integral part of the disease and a major obstacle to recovery.[LXXII]

Appendix B

TREATMENT OPTIONS FREQUENTLY USED TO TREAT ALCOHOLISM

Generally the successful treatment of alcoholism [defined as remission, not a cure] involves some combination of the following:

- Individual therapy ("talk therapy") with a Ph.D. in psychology, MFT (Marriage, Family Therapist), LCSW (Licensed Clinical Social Worker) or CDAS (Certified Drug and Alcohol Specialist) who is trained in addictions and who has extensive experience working with alcoholics.

- Medication – there are new ones, now, that effectively work to combat the cravings for alcohol, which allows the recovering alcoholic to focus on overcoming other aspects of the disease, such as the cues associated with drinking.

- Residential (live at the treatment center) or out-patient (live at home and go to the treatment center during days or evenings) alcohol treatment programs with long-term after care and follow-up. [Appendix C offers suggestions on "What to Look for in a Residential or Out-patient Treatment Program."]

- Cognitive-behavior therapy – the same kinds of specialists described under "talk therapy" help the alcoholic to look at what triggers and reinforces the cues to drink and helps them identify methods of short-circuiting the process – such as teaching the alcoholic how to stop the urge to drink when they hear the cork pop by thinking of something else, instead, with the "something else instead" being worked out in therapy.

- Alcoholics Anonymous (AA) – a 12-step program. Often reading or hearing about steps 1 (admitted we were powerless over alcohol) and 3 (came to believe in a power greater than our own [a "higher power"]) puts people off initially. The idea behind the 1st step is that the alcoholic's way of "white-knuckling"[1] their urge to drink did not work, so they need to reach out at those particular times for help instead of insisting they have the "power" to control it. The idea behind the "higher power" is to look to something beyond one's self – that could be "God" in a religious sense or the wisdom of those in an AA meeting or a giant redwood in one's backyard. AA (and other 12-step programs) are not religious; agnostics and atheists are more than welcome. AA is about alcoholics sharing what works for them with no judgment or expectation of what others should or should not be doing. Other aspects of AA include regularly attending meetings,[2] having a sponsor (someone who has been in the AA program and whose recovery the alcoholic admires) – the sponsor is available to answer questions, help them work the steps, be the one they call when they have an urge to drink, etc.[3]

- Exercise / yoga / meditation—something positive the alcoholic does for their health that also takes their mind away from the battle with self not to drink.

- An Intervention - basically a carefully planned group meeting, best led by a professional substance abuse counselor, in which family members, friends, and employers tell the alcoholic how his or her drinking has been a problem in their lives. Then the alcoholic is offered an opportunity to get treatment.

- Other similar programs / treatment options and/or faith-based beliefs and practices – whatever it takes to learn how to manage the cues and cravings (the triggers) and to stop the denial.

Alcoholics in recovery often have family members involved at some level in the process, as well. This might include reading a book like this one, seeking their own counseling/therapy and/or participation in a 12-step program for family and friends of alcoholics (Al-Anon or Alateen). [Appendix G presents a description of programs that have proved to be of great help to family members of alcoholics.]

---

[1] a metaphorical statement for someone sitting in a chair, gripping the arms of the chair (white knuckles), desperately trying not to drink.

[2] There's a saying, "90 in 90," and it refers to the suggestion that newly recovering alcoholics should attend 90 meetings in 90 days – 1 meeting per day.

[3] A note of caution here: there is no "right way" to do a 12-step program. Some simply attend meetings and do nothing else, some have sponsors and some don't. Some work the steps once, others work them over and over, and still others never work them yet do attend the meetings. Many alcoholics use AA initially and then become more involved in their church or spiritual / faith-based beliefs and practices, instead. There's an expression used in the meeting closings: "Take What You Like and Leave the Rest." That about sums it up.

One Day at a Time

This is one of the AA slogans. It refers to the notion of staying sober one day at a time. When a person thinks of "never drinking for the rest of their life" – that can seem to be an overwhelming challenge. But, if they think of not drinking, just for today, that can seem achievable.

For More Information About Recovery from Alcoholism

Alcoholics Anonymous (AA) World Services • http://www.aa.org

> Makes referrals to local AA groups and provides informational materials on the AA program. Many cities and towns also have a local AA office listed in the telephone book.

National Council on Alcoholism and Drug Dependence (NCADD) • http://www.ncadd.org

> Provides telephone numbers of local NCADD affiliates (who can provide information on local treatment resources) and educational materials on alcoholism.

Treatment Centers • www.treatment-centers.net

> This web site offers information on alcoholism and dual diagnosis and a comprehensive directory of over 8,000 drug and alcohol treatment centers, drug rehabs and alcohol rehabilitation programs, and mental health treatment centers.

Appendix C

WHAT TO LOOK FOR IN A RESIDENTIAL OR OUT-PATIENT TREATMENT PROGRAM FOR ALCOHOLISM

The U.S. Department of Health and Human Services' Substance Abuse and Mental Health Services Administration's Center for Substance Abuse Treatment (CSAT) offers a number of questions alcoholics should consider when selecting a residential or out-patient treatment program. The following CSAT questions are shared to help you understand what the experts consider effective treatment.

1. Is there ongoing assessment of an individual's treatment plan to ensure it meets changing needs?

2. Does the program employ strategies to engage and keep individuals in longer-term treatment, increasing the likelihood of success?

3. Does the program offer counseling (individual or group) and other behavioral therapies to enhance the individual's ability to function in the family/community?

4. Does the program offer medication as part of the treatment regimen, if appropriate?

5. Is there ongoing monitoring of possible relapse to help guide patients back to abstinence?

6. Are services or referrals offered to family members to ensure they understand addiction and the recovery process to help them support the recovering individual?

7. Do those same family services address the needs of each family member? Their recovery as co-dependents is equally as important as the recovery of the alcoholic.

CSAT has a 24-hour help line, 1-800-662-HELP, for treatment options near you. Again, this is offered only to help you gather further information for your own understanding. It is not meant as something you should use to get your loved one to do something to stop their drinking.

For more information:

"A Quick Guide to Finding Effective Alcohol and Drug Addiction Treatment," Center for Substance Abuse Treatment (CSAT),< http://csat.samhsa.gov/faqs.aspx>

Appendix D

CODEPENDENCY ASSESSMENT #2

This list has been adapted with permission from one used by The Sequoia Center, an alcohol and drug treatment center. Mark (A) agree or (D) disagree as your read through the following statements. There is no scoring, however your answers will give you an idea of the types of codependent coping skills you've adopted in order to survive.

___ My good feelings about who I am stem from being liked by others.

___ My good feelings about who I am stem from receiving approval from others.

___ Another's struggle affects my serenity. My mental attention focuses on solving their problems or relieving their pain.

___ My mental attention is focused on pleasing others.

___ My mental attention is focused on protecting others.

___ My mental attention is focused on manipulating others (to do it my way) because I have their best interests at heart.

_____ My self-esteem is bolstered by solving another's problems.

_____ My self-esteem is bolstered by relieving another's pain.

_____ My own hobbies and interests are put aside; my time is spent sharing another's interests and hobbies.

_____ Another's clothing and personal appearance are dictated by my desires, as I feel they are a reflection of me.

_____ Another's behavior is dictated by my desires, as I feel they are a reflection of me.

_____ I am not aware of how I feel. I am aware of how others feel.

_____ I am not aware of what I want – I ask what others want. I am not aware – I assume.

_____ The dreams I have for my future are linked to another's.

_____ My fear of rejection determines what I say or do.

_____ My fear of another's anger determines what I say or do.

_____ I use giving as a way of feeling safe in relationships.

_____ My social circle diminishes as I involve myself with the alcoholic.

_____ I value others' opinions and ways of doing things more than my own.

_____ The quality of my life is in relation to the quality of another's.

Appendix E

SLOGANS AND SAYINGS TO HELP YOU MOVE FROM "REACTING" TO "RESPONDING"

Al-Anon, Alateen, AA and other recovery-type programs offer a wide array of slogans, phrases and sayings, as have many people throughout the centuries. I use these as thoughts to anchor my "thinking" when I feel myself losing control. I've written them on post-it notes and stuck them on my mirror or on a cupboard door or on the dash of my car to remind me there's an alternative to my "crazy" thinking (the thinking that takes hold without thinking because it's so ingrained). [P.S. They work whether dealing with an alcoholic, alcohol abuser _or_ someone else.] Here are some of my favorites:

HALT. **Hungry, Angry [and I've added Anxious], Lonely or Tired.**

> Stop everything and regroup. HAALT is one of my favorite slogans to help with this. Ask yourself, "Am I hungry, angry, anxious, lonely or tired?" Generally, I've found when I HAALT at the first sense of that unsettled feeling, I can get to the real source of my anxiety, which very often is not what I thought it was. Then, I can deal with the source issue appropriately – such as stopping to eat, calling a friend, taking a nap or figuring out exactly what I'm angry or anxious about. If I don't, then I usually make things worse because I've done something

like rush my daughter through something we'd planned together because my thoughts are consumed with being mad at Alex.

One Day at a Time

And for me, this has boiled down to the next 5 minutes at a time. It's the idea that no matter how bad it may be, you just have to get through one day (or 5 minutes) and somehow that makes it seem achievable.

"I have been through some terrible things in my life, some of which actually happened."

— Mark Twain

This one speaks to the futility of worrying about what may or may not happen.

Anger is one letter away from danger

I've had a heck of a lot of it and now use this slogan to help pull me back from the insanity that overwhelms me when I give in to being angry.

Fear is the darkroom where negatives are developed

I use this to keep me from giving into the panic caused by the unknown. I used to have intense fear of the unknown and could not take action because I didn't have all the answers or know all of the possible outcomes – "what if . . ." was my common refrain. Now I don't let fear dictate what I do or don't do.

If you don't like what you feel, change what you think.

Yes, we really do have absolute power over what we think. We can think whatever we want to think, thus we can feel however we want to feel. One of the things I do when I keep getting the same negative thought(s) over and over [especially when I'm dealing with a problem that takes time to correct, for example] is to literally say, "Stop." And when the thought pops in again (and again), I jar my thinking with "Stop" and replace the problem-related thoughts with ones about something good in my life, or I'll force myself to notice my surroundings and focus on those. This only works, of course, if I've taken time to think through the problem and know I'm doing what I can do about it at that particular time. If I'm really wound up, I set aside time to look at my "worry list" (which can be in my head, but better if it's on paper), decide if I've done what I can do for that day about those worries, and then choose to think of something else, instead. I can miss the entire day, otherwise.

Patience

Just as it likely took you a long time to get to this point, it will take time to change your behaviors. Be patient with yourself and count every time you do it differently as a success – even if you slip again tomorrow.

Second Half of the Serenity Prayer

The first half of the prayer is most familiar, but I really like the second half, as well:

> *Grant me Patience for the things that take time,*
> *Appreciation for all that I have,*
> *Tolerance for others with different struggles, and the*
> *Strength to get up and try again, one day at a time.*

Every accomplishment begins with a decision to try.　　　　　— Edward T. Kelly

Don't wait until you have all the answers or an assured outcome before you start

Let It Go

I had no idea how to do this in the beginning. I would talk about something that was really upsetting and do what I needed to do to come to terms with it, but then it was like a kite on a string. I'd let it go, but it'd be still be up "there" floating – like a kite on a string (not as much on my mind as before, but it was still there). Finally I started to think of "letting go" as using a scissors to cut the string and watch the kite fly away.

Fear is the darkened hallway. Faith is the lighted door.

I clung to this idea that if I just moved towards the lighted door and focused on that, I could make it through the darkened hallway (my metaphor for whatever I was grappling with at the time).

Appendix F

CHANGE WHAT YOU THINK AND YOU'LL CHANGE HOW YOU FEEL

Cognitive Restructuring Using Grammatical [Polar] Opposites

One of the key issues for codependents is to stop seeing life in absolutes – all good / all bad; all right / all wrong – because a distortion occurs simply by virtue of the absolutes (the grammatical opposites). When you replace an absolute with a realistic thought, the distortion goes away, which allows you to think of a response that will work for you.

The following exercise is a form of Cognitive Behavioral Therapy (CBT), which is designed to give you the opportunity to move from your typical reaction to a more reasoned response. I've adapted it a bit to use some of what worked for me in the beginning – namely, to think of the polar (grammatical) opposite to my first reaction or thought. Then, I look at them both, which makes it easier to see the "appropriate" response, because, as I've gotten more solid in my recovery, I find it's usually somewhere between the two.

In this example, the trigger is a phone call to a mother from her alcoholic daughter:

1. Identify the upsetting event.
(My daughter called and talked on and on about how she was really broke and had her rent due and needed gas money.)

2. Identify your feelings.
(Mad, sad, anxious, guilty.)

3. Identify your first reaction.
(Oh my gosh. I think I can spare $200. I can't let her lose her apartment. Where would she live?)

4. What is the grammatical [polar] opposite of your first reaction?
(No way am I going to send her money. She's an adult. If she'd stop drinking, she could hang onto a job and have plenty of money.)*

5. Then, ask yourself, "How do I feel?"
(Calmer but still sad her drinking gets in her way of keeping a job. I love her so much; it breaks my heart to see her like this but giving her money hasn't worked, either.)

6. Now, ask yourself, "How do I want to respond?"
(I'm not going to comment when she talks about being broke – just listen without judgment. I've told her before what I think, but I can't keep rescuing her, either.)

Remember: "Respond," don't "React" (see Chapter 7).

For more information about this idea (and the "official way" it's used), you may want to read David D. Burns, M.D., *The Feeling Good Handbook*. Take this concept a step further and read *Mind Set* by Carol S. Dweck, Ph.D.

Appendix G

The following are other kinds of outside help suggestions that have worked for hundreds of thousands of people who love an alcoholic or alcohol abuser (excessive drinker):

* Individual therapy ("talk therapy") with a Ph.D. in psychology, MFT (Marriage, Family Therapist) or LCSW (Licensed Clinical Social Worker) who has extensive experience working with the family members of alcoholics and alcohol abusers. Seeing a therapist with this kind of experience is critical because they will understand the issues surrounding addiction, alcohol abuse, adult children of alcoholics (ACAs), co-addictions, codependency and the like.

* Cognitive-behavior therapy – this looks at what triggers and reinforces the cues to your automatic reactions and looks for methods of short-circuiting or changing them to thinking-type responses. [See Appendix F for an example.]

* Group counseling or workshops – meeting in groups with others whose relative or friend is an alcoholic or abuses alcohol (provided it is led by someone with extensive experience understanding alcoholism, alcohol abuse and codependency) is a huge help – primarily to learn you're not alone and then to bounce ideas off one another. This kind of gathering is somewhat different than a 12-step program described next because it allows what is called "cross-talk" – the ability to talk to another person in the group and/or comment on what they've said. In a 12-step program meeting, cross talk is not allowed.

* Al-Anon – a 12-step program for the family and friends of alcoholics and alcohol abusers – the only "criteria" is there be a problem of alcohol. There is also Alateen for teens. Often reading or hearing about steps 1 (admitted we were powerless over alcohol [over whether or not a loved one drinks]) and 3 (came to believe in a power greater than our own [a "higher power"]) puts people off, initially. It did for me because I didn't understand what it meant. For now, I say, go and see what happens. There's no timeline – no "right way" to do Al-Anon. It is not a religious program (atheists and agnostics are more than welcome). Basically, Al-Anon (and other 12-step programs) are about people sharing what works for them, with no judgment or expectation of what others should or should not be doing. [There are Al-Anon meetings specifically for parents of alcoholics, too, which can be especially helpful to those whose child is the loved one who drinks too much.]

* Exercise / yoga / meditation – something positive that you can do for your health that helps shift your focus from the alcoholic/alcohol abuser. Anything that allows you to focus on yourself helps you to stop trying to control the

alcoholic's or the alcohol abuser's drinking (or the alcoholic's recovery, alcohol abuser's alcohol use or the lives of your non-drinking loved ones and friends, for that matter).

- Other similar programs/treatment options and/or faith-based beliefs and practices – whatever it takes to learn how to stop the denial and to manage your reactions and how to set appropriate boundaries.

Only when you're ready – this has been repeatedly stated – but it's important to know that you do what you can when you're ready. Recovery from codependent coping skills and behaviors takes time. Often what is needed in the beginning changes or lessens as you become more confident and comfortable with your real self.

For More Information About Help With Codependency

Adult Children of Alcoholics Worldwide Service Organization • www.adultchildren.org/Contact.s
For adult children (and grandchildren, nieces, nephews) of an alcoholic.

Al-Anon Family Group Headquarters • www.al-anon.alateen.org.
Makes referrals to local Al-Anon groups, which are support groups for spouses and other significant adults in an alcoholic person's life. Also makes referrals to Alateen groups, which offer support to children of alcoholics.

Alateen • www.al-anon.alateen.org
Alateen is similar to Al-Anon and is the 12-step recovery program for young people.

Brown, Stephanie, Ph.D. and Virginia Lewis, Ph.D., *The Alcoholic Family in Recovery, a Developmental Model*, New York: The Gilford Press, 1999.

Brown, Stephanie, Ph.D. and Virginia M. Lewis, Ph.D., with Andrew Lioitta, *The Family Recovery Guide, A Map for Healthy Growth*, Oakland, CA: New Harbinger Publications, Inc., 2000.

How Al-Anon Works for Families & Friends of Alcoholics (Al-Anon Family Groups 1995).

Bibliography

"The Addiction Project," Home Box Office, Inc. (HBO) in partnership with the Robert Wood Johnson Foundation, the NIAAA and the NIDA (National Institute on Drug Abuse), Home Box Office, Inc.: March 2007, <http://www.hbo.com/addiction/>

Al-Anon Family Groups, "Al-Anon Faces Alcoholism 2007, Are You Troubled by Someone's Drinking?" Virginia Beach, VA: Al-Anon Family Group Headquarters, Inc., 2006.

Al-Anon Family Groups, *How Al-Anon Works, For Families & Friends of Alcoholics*. Virginia Beach, VA: Al-Anon Family Group Headquarters, Inc., 1995.

"Alcohol Abuse Diagnosis," Mental Health Channel, <http://www.mentalhealthchannel.net/alcohol/diagnosis.shtml>

"Alcohol's Damaging Effects on the Brain," NIAAA of the National Institutes of Health, Publication Number 63, October 2004, <http://pubs.niaaa.nih.gov/publications/aa63/aa63.htm>

"Alcohol and Drug Abuse, Addiction and Co-Occurring Disorders," National Mental Health Association (NMHA), 2007, <http://www1.nmha.org/substance/advocate.cfm>

"All About MRI [PET, DTI]," Laboratory for Science at Dartmouth College, <http://theteenbrain.com/takepart/MRI/#dtilong>

Amen, Daniel, M.D., "Which Brain Do You Want?" (DVD), Amen Clinics, 2004.

Babor, Thomas F. and John C. Higgins-Biddle, John B. Saunders and Maristela G. Monteiro, "AUDIT (The Alcohol Use Disorders Identification Test)," World Health Organization (WHO), Department of Mental Health and Substance Dependence, Second Edition, 2001, <http://whqlibdoc.who.int/hq/2001/WHO_MSD_MSB_01.6a.pdf >

Beattie, Melody, *Codependent No More, How to Stop Controlling Others and Start Caring For Yourself*, Center City, MN: Hazelden, 1992.

Black, Claudia, Ph.D., *Straight Talk From Claudia Black, What Recovering Parents Should Tell Their Kids About Drugs and Alcohol*, Center City, MN: Hazelden, 2003.

Boggan, Bill, Dr., "Alcohol, Chemistry and You, Effects of Ethyl Alcohol on Organ Function," Kennesaw State University, 2003, <http://www.chemcases.com/alcohol/alc-07.htm>

Brown, Stephanie and Virginia Lewis, *The Alcoholic Family in Recovery, A Developmental Model*, New York: The Guilford Press, 1999.

Brown, Stephanie Brown, Ph.D. and Virginia M. Lewis, Ph.D., *The Family Recovery Guide, A Map for Healthy Growth*, Oakland, CA: New Harbinger Publications, Inc., 2000.

Carey, Joseph, Editor, "Brain Facts, A Primer on the Brain and Nervous System," Washington, D.C., Society for Neuroscience, 2005, 2006, <www.sfn.org>, go to *Publications*, click on *Brain Facts*.

Childress, Anna Rose, Ph.D., "Let's Talk About Craving," HBO.com/addiction: March 2007, <http://www.hbo.com/addiction/understanding_addiction/13_craving.html>

"Codependency," Mental Health America (formerly known as the National Mental Health Association), <http://www.mentalhealthamerica.net/go/codependency>

Committee on Developing a Strategy to Reduce and Prevent Underage Drinking, National Research Council Institute of Medicine of the National Academies, *Reducing Underage Drinking, A Collective Responsibility*, Washington, D.C.: The National Academies Press, 2004.

Crowley, Thomas, M.D. and Elizabeth Whitmore, Ph.D, "Five Things to Know About Adolescents' Brain Development and Use," HBO.com/addiction: March 2007, <http://www.hbo.com/addiction/adolescent_addiction/21_adolescent_brain_development.html>

Dweck, Carol S., Ph.D., Mind Set, The New Psychology of Success, *How We Can Learn to Fulfill Our Potential*, New York: Ballentine Books, 2006.

Drews, Toby Rice, *Getting Them Sober, You Can Help!, Vol. 1, 3rd Edition*. Baltimore, Maryland: Recovery Communications, Inc., 1994.

Goodwin, Donald W., *Alcoholism: the Facts, 3rd Edition*, New York: Oxford University Press, 2000.

Hutt, Jim, Ph.D., "Alcohol, Drugs & Adolescent Brain Development," Menlo Atherton High School, PTA – F.A.C.T.S. (Focus on Alcohol – Committee for Teen Safety), March 2006.

Ketcham, Katherine and William F. Asbury, *Beyond the Influence, Understanding and Defeating Alcoholism*, New York: Bantam Books, 2000.

Kotulak, Ronald, *Inside the Brain: Revolutionary Discoveries of How the Mind Works*, Kansas City, Missouri: Andrews McMeel Publishing, 1996.

Lemonick, Michael D. with Alice Park, "The Science of Addiction," TIME, July 16, 2007, Time, Inc.. pgs. 42-48.

Maxwell, Ruth, *BREAKTHROUGH, What to Do when Alcoholism or Chemical Dependency Hits Close to Home*, New York: Ballantine Books, 1986.

National Institute on Alcohol Abuse and Alcoholism (NIAAA), U.S. Department of Health and Human Services, National Institutes of Health, "Alcoholism, Getting the Facts," NIH Publication No. 96-4153, Revised 2004.

National Institutes of Health, National Institute on Drug Abuse (NIDA), "Drugs, Brains, and Behavior – The Science of Addiction, " <http://www.drugabuse.gov/scienceofaddiction/> specifically, "Drugs and the Brain," <http://www.drugabuse.gov/scienceofaddiction/brain.html>

Neimark, Neil F., M.D., "The Fight or Flight Response," Mind/Body Education Center, <http://www.thebodysoulconnection.com/EducationCenter/fight.html>

Perry, Bruce D., M.D., Ph.D., B*rain Structure and Function, Basics of Organization*, adapted in part from: "Maltreated Children: Experience, Brain Development and the Next Generation," (W.W. Norton & Company, NY), Houston, TX: ChildTrauma Academy, 2002, <www.ChildTrauma.org>

Phelps, M.D., James R., "Your '3-Brains-in-One' Brain," Corvallis, OR: PyschEducation.org, 2000-2007, http://www.psycheducation.org/emotion/triune%20brain.htm>

Rosenbloom, Margaret, M.A. and Edith V. Sullivan Ph.D. and Adolf Pfefferbaum, M.D., "Using Magnetic Resonance Imaging and Diffusion Tensor Imaging to Assess Brain Damage in Alcoholics," NIAAA of the National Institutes of Health, 2004.

Stufflebeam, Robert, "Neurons, Synapses, and Neurotransmission: An Introduction," Normal, IL: The Mind / Brain Project, Consortium on Mind/Brain Science Instruction, 2006, <http://www.mind.ilstu.edu/ curriculum/neurons_intro/neurons_intro.php>

Thorburn, Doug, *Alcoholism Myths and Realities: Removing the Stigma of Society's Most Destructive Disease*, Northridge, CA: Galt Publishing, 2005.

Typpo, Marion H., Ph.D and Jill M. Hastings, Ph.D., *An Elephant in the Living Room*, Center City, MN: Hazelden, 1984.

U.S. Department of Health & Human Services, National Institutes of Health (NIH), National Institute on Alcohol Abuse and Alcoholism (NIAAA)'s 2005, Clinician's Guide, "Helping Patients Who Drink Too Much," NIAAA: 2005, <http://www.niaaa.nih.gov/Publications/EducationTrainingMaterials/guide.htm>

United States Department of Health and Human Services (HHS) and the U.S. Department of Agriculture (USDA), "Dietary Guidelines for Americans 2005, Chapter 9, 'Alcoholic Beverages,'" USDA/HHS: Updated 2/05/07, <http://www.health.gov/dietaryguidelines/dga2005/document/html/chapter9.htm>

Volkow, Nora D., M.D., "Addiction and the Brain's Pleasure Pathway: Beyond Willpower," HBO.com/addiction: March 2007, <http://www.hbo.com/addiction/understanding_addiction/12_pleasure_pathway.html>

World Health Organization (WHO), "AUDIT (The Alcohol Use Disorders Identification Test)," <http://whqlibdoc.who.int/hq/2001/WHO_MSD_MSB_01.6a.pdf >

Endnotes

Chapter 1

[i] World Health Organization (WHO), "AUDIT (The Alcohol Use Disorders Identification Test)," page 5, <http://whqlibdoc.who.int/hq/2001/WHO_MSD_MSB_01.6a.pdf >

Chapter 2

[ii] World Health Organization (WHO), "AUDIT, (The Alcohol Use Disorders Identification Test)," page 6, <http://whqlibdoc.who.int/hq/2001/WHO_MSD_MSB_01.6a.pdf >

[iii] USDA, "Dietary Guidelines for Americans 2005, Chapter 9: Alcoholic Beverages," <http://www.health.gov/dietaryguidelines/dga2005/document/html/chapter9.htm>

[iv] U.S. Department of Health & Human Services, National Institutes of Health (NIH), National Institute on Alcohol Abuse and Alcoholism (NIAAA), "Helping Patients Who Drink Too Much, A Clinician's Guide," 2005, <http://www.niaaa.nih.gov/Publications/EducationTrainingMaterials/guide.htm>

[v] USDA Dietary Guidelines for Americans 2005.

[vi] U.S. Department of Health & Human Services, National Institutes of Health (NIH), National Institute on Alcohol Abuse and Alcoholism (NIAAA), "How to Help Patients Who Drink Too Much, A Clinical Approach," 2005, http://pubs.niaaa.nih.gov/publications/Practitioner/CliniciansGuide2005/clinicians_guide5_help_p.htm>

[vii] World Health Organization (WHO), "AUDIT," page 2, <http://whqlibdoc.who.int/hq/2001/WHO_MSD MSB_01.6a.pdf >

[viii] *Ibid.*, pgs. 17, 19 and 20.

[ix] *Ibid.*, pgs. 5-6.

[x] "Alcohol Abuse Diagnosis," Mental Health Channel, <http://www.mentalhealthchannel.net/alcohol/diagnosis.shtml>

[xi] "Definition of Alcoholism," National Council on Alcoholism and Drug Dependence (NCADD), <http://www.ncadd.org/facts/defalc.html>

[xii] "Alcohol Abuse Diagnosis," Mental Health Channel, <http://www.mentalhealthchannel.net/alcohol/diagnosis.shtml>

[xiii] "Understanding Addiction," HBO.com/addiction: March 2007, <http://www.hbo.com/addiction/understanding_addiction/index.html?current=0>

Chapter 3

[xiv] Carey, Joseph, Editor, "Brain Facts, A Primer on the Brain and Nervous System," Washington, D.C., Society for Neuroscience, 2005, 2006, <www.sfn.org>, go to Publications, click on Brain Facts, p. 36.

[xv] *Ibid.*

[xvi] Stufflebeam, Robert, "Neurons, Synapses, and Neurotransmission: An Introduction," Normal, IL: The Mind/Brain Project, Consortium on Mind/Brain Science Instruction, 2006, pgs. 1-2, <http://www.mind.ilstu.edu/curriculum/neurons_intro/neurons_intro.php>

[xvii] Carey, Joseph, Editor, "Brain Facts, A Primer on the Brain and Nervous System."

[xviii] "Neurons and Their Jobs," U.S. National Institutes of Health, National Institute on Aging, <http://www.nia.nih.gov/Alzheimers/Publications/UnravelingTheMystery/Part1/NeuronsAndTheirJobs.htm>

[xix] Carey, Joseph, Editor, "Brain Facts, A Primer on the Brain and Nervous System," p. 6.

[xx] Hutt, Jim, Ph.D., "Alcohol, Drugs & Adolescent Brain Development."

[xxi] Childress, Anna Rose, Ph.D. "Let's Talk About Craving," HBO.com/addiction: March 2007, <http://www.hbo.com/addiction/understanding_addiction/13_craving.html>

[xxii] Kotulak, Ronald, "Inside the Brain: Revolutionary Discoveries of How the Mind Works," Kansas City, Missouri: Andrews McMeel Publishing, 1996, p. 110; AND Carey, Joseph, Editor, "Brain Facts, A Primer on the Brain and Nervous System," Washington, D.C., Society for Neuroscience, 2005, 2006, <www.sfn.org>, go to Publications, click on Brain Facts, pg. 36.

[xxiii] Volkow, Nora D., M.D., "Addiction and the Brain's Pleasure Pathway: Beyond Willpower," HBO.com/addiction: March 2007, <http://www.hbo.com/addiction/understanding_addiction/12_pleasure_pathway.html>

[xxiv] Ibid.

[xxv] Ibid.

[xxvi] "Drugs and the Brain," National Institutes of Health, National Institute on Drug Abuse (NIDA), <http://www.drugabuse.gov/scienceofaddiction/brain.html>

[xxvii] Ibid.

[xxviii] Childress, Anna Rose, Ph.D., "Let's Talk About Craving."

[xxix] Ibid.

[xxx] Ibid.

[xxxi] "Why Do Some People Become Addicted?" HBO.com/addiction: March 2007, <www.hbo.com/addiction>, AND "Drugs and the Brain," National Institutes of Health, National Institute on Drug Abuse (NIDA), <http://www.drugabuse.gov/scienceofaddiction/brain.html>

[xxxii] "Drug Abuse and Addiction," National Institute on Drug Abuse (IDA), National Institutes of Health, <http://www.nida.nih.gov/scienceofaddiction/addiction.html>

[xxxiii] Lemonick, Michael D. with Alice Park, "The Science of Addiction," TIME, July 16, 2007, Time, Inc.. p. 46.

[xxxiv] Why Do Some People Become Addicted?" HBO.com/addiction: March 2007, www.hbo.com/addiction, AND "Drugs and the Brain," National Institutes of Health, National Institute on Drug Abuse (NIDA), <http://www.drugabuse.gov/scienceofaddiction/brain.html>

[xxxv] Ibid.

[xxxvi] "Alcoholism, Getting the Facts," National Institute on Alcohol Abuse and Alcoholism (NIAAA), U.S. Department of Health and Human Services, National Institutes of Health, NIH Publication No. 96-4153, Revised 2004, pg. 3.

[xxxvii] Moritsugu, Kenneth, M.D., M.P.H., "Acting U.S. Surgeon General Issues National Call to Action on Underage Drinking," U.S. Department of Health and Human Services, <http://www.hhs.gov/news/press/2007pres/20070306.html>

[xxxviii] Crowley, Thomas, M.D. and Elizabeth Whitmore, Ph.D., "Five Things to Know About Adolescents' Brain Development and Use," HBO.com/addiction: March 2007, <http://www.hbo.com/addiction/adolescent_addiction/21_adolescent_brain_development.html>

[xxxix] Hutt, Jim, Ph.D.,"Alcohol, Drugs & Adolescent Brain Development."

[xl] Ibid.

[xli] Ibid.

[xlii] Crowley, Thomas, M.D. and Elizabeth Whitmore, Ph.D., "Five Things to Know About Adolescents' Brain Development and Use."

Chapter 4

[XLIII] Brown, Stephanie, Ph.D. and Virginia M. Lewis, Ph.D., with Andrew Liotta, *The Family Recovery Guide, A Map for Healthy Growth*, Oakland, CA: New Harbinger Publications, Inc., 2000., p. 34.

[XLIV] *Ibid.*, pgs 34–35.

[XLV] Sources include: Maxwell, Ruth, *BREAKTHROUGH, What to do When Alcoholism or Chemical Dependency Hits Close to Home,"* New York: Ballantine Books, 1986, pgs. 63-75, and Brown, Stephanie, Ph.D. and Virginia M. Lewis, Ph.D., with Andrew Liotta, *The Family Recovery Guide, A Map for Healthy Growth*, Oakland, CA: New Harbinger Publications, Inc., 2000, pgs. various throughout.

[XLVI] Volkow, Nora D., M.D., "Addiction and the Brain's Pleasure Pathway: Beyond Willpower."

[XLVII] Brown, Stephanie, Ph.D. and Virginia M. Lewis, Ph.D., with Andrew Liotta, p. 3.

[XLVIII] Shaw, Brian F., Ph.D. and Paul Ritvo, Ph.D. and Jane Irvine, *Addiction & Recovery for Dummies*, Hoboken, NJ: Wiley Publishing, Inc., 2005, pp. 229-230.

[XLIX] Volkow, Nora D., M.D., "Addiction and the Brain's Pleasure Pathway: Beyond Willpower."

[L] Willenbring, M.D., Mark L. , "An APA [American Psychiatric Association] Expert Answers Common Questions About Alcohol Awareness Month," American Psychiatric Association, HealthyMinds.org, <http://www.healthy-minds.org/expertopinion11.cfm>

[LI] Volkow, Nora D., M.D., "Addiction and the Brain's Pleasure Pathway: Beyond Willpower," HBO.com/addiction: March 2007, http://www.hbo.com/addiction/understanding_addiction/12_pleasure_pathway.html

[LII] *Ibid.*

[LIII] HBO.com/addiction,<http://www.hbo.com/addiction/understanding_addiction/142_co-occurring_disorders.html>

[LIV] *Ibid.*

[LV] *Ibid.*

[LVI] HBO.com/addiction, <http://www.hbo.com/addiction/understanding_addiction/12_pleasure_pathway.html>

[LVII] *Ibid.*

Chapter 5

[LVIII] Brown, Stephanie, Ph.D. and Virginia M. Lewis, Ph.D., with Andrew Liotta, *The Family Recovery Guide, A Map for Healthy Growth*, Oakland, CA: New Harbinger Publications, Inc., 2000, p. 3.

[LIX] *Ibid.*

[LX] "Codependency," Mental Health America (formerly known as the National Mental Health Association), <http://www.mentalhealthamerica.net/go/codependency>

[LXI] *Ibid.*

[LXII] *Ibid.*

[LXIII] *Ibid.*

Chapter 6

[LXIV] Brown, Stephanie, Ph.D. and Virginia M. Lewis, Ph.D., with Andrew Liotta, *The Family Recovery Guide, A Map for Healthy Growth*, Oakland, CA: New Harbinger Publications, Inc., 2000, p. 3.

[LXV] Neimark, Neil F., M.D., "The Fight or Flight Response," Mind/Body Education Center, <http://www.thebodysoulconnection.com/EducationCenter/fight.html>

[LXVI] Sources for these are varied and include: Brown, Stephanie, Ph.D. and Virginia M. Lewis, Ph.D., with Andrew Liotta, *The Family Recovery Guide, A Map for Healthy Growth*, Oakland, CA: New Harbinger Publications, Inc., 2000, AND Maxwell, Ruth, *BREAKTHROUGH, What to Do when Alcoholism or Chemical Dependency Hits Close to Home*, New York: Ballantine Books, 1986, AND The Sequoia Center, AND Dr. James Hutt, AND the hundreds of codependents in recovery programs I've spoken with.

[LXVII] *Ibid.*

Chapter 7

[LXVIII] Sources for these are varied and include: Brown, Stephanie, Ph.D. and Virginia M. Lewis, Ph.D., with Andrew Liotta, *The Family Recovery Guide, A Map for Healthy Growth*, Oakland, CA: New Harbinger Publications, Inc., 2000, AND Maxwell, Ruth, *BREAKTHROUGH, What to Do when Alcoholism or Chemical Dependency Hits Close to Home*, New York: Ballantine Books, 1986, AND The Sequoia Center, AND Dr. James Hutt, AND the hundreds of codependents in recovery programs I've spoken with.

[LXIX] Brown, Stephanie, Ph.D. and Virginia M. Lewis, Ph.D., with Andrew Liotta, p. 7.

[LXX] Sources for these are varied and include: Brown, Stephanie, Ph.D. . . . .

Chapter 8

[LXXI] Al-Anon Family Groups, "Al-Anon Faces Alcoholism 2007, Are You Troubled by Someone's Drinking?" Virginia Beach, VA: Al-Anon Family Group Headquarters, Inc. 2006.

Appendix A-7

[LXXII] "Definition of Alcoholism," National Council on Alcoholism and Drug Dependence (NCADD), <http://www.ncadd.org/facts/defalc.html>